The Beauty of the
Disciplined Life
by Grace through Faith

Blessings!
2023

Deidre Bobgan

Except where otherwise indicated, all Scripture quotations in this book are taken from the New American Standard Bible, © The Lockman Foundation 1960, 1962, 1963, 1968, 1971 , 1972, 1973, 1975, 1977. Used by permission given to the original publication of this book, formerly titled *Lord of the Dance*, 1987.

Verses marked KJV are taken from the King James Version of the Bible.

The Beauty of the Disciplined Life by Grace through Faith

This work is a republishing of *The Lord of the Dance*, originally published by Harvest House, 1987.

Copyright © 2017 Deidre Bobgan
Published by EastGate Publishers
Santa Barbara, CA 93110

Library of Congress Control Number 2017959508
ISBN 978-0941717-26-7

With love and gratitude to Martin,
my husband, friend, and encourager
in the Lord.

About the Author

The Beauty of the Disciplined Life by Grace through Faith (2017) was originally published in 1987 under the title *Lord of the Dance: The Beauty of the Disciplined Life.* The content is the same. Only the title has changed.

Deidre Bobgan studied ballet for twelve years, earned a bachelor's degree in Theatre Arts and a master's degree in English. She is a member of the honorary academic society Phi Beta Kappa. Through the years she has enjoyed ministering to women and speaking to women's groups. Deidre and her husband, Martin, have four children, ten grandchildren and three great-grandchildren. Together Martin and Deidre developed and directed a personal care ministry in their church and have coauthored 23 books and over 300 articles.

Preface

Thirty years have passed since the first publication of this book under the title *Lord of the Dance*. My body has aged through those years, yet my spirit continues to soar in Christ who is my Life and who has been faithful through these many years. As I re-read this book I was drawn closer to the Lord and was also renewed in my appreciation for the discipline required for excellence in art, music, drama, dance, literature, sports, education, or any other worthy endeavor that requires dedication and humility. I was further inspired by renewing my acquaintance with *Ballet Magnificat!* which is highlighted at the end of this book.

Paul described aspects of the Christian life with those of boxing and running. In this book I am following his example, but with an extended analogy using ballet instead of boxing or running. The similarities of walking by grace through faith in the Lord Jesus Christ and becoming an accomplished artist, musician, actor, dancer, writer, athlete, or educator highlight indispensable attitudes and actions. Excellence requires dedication and humility as instruction, correction, change, and practice are inevitable necessities in the development of a dancer, musician, athlete, or writer, no matter how talented a person may be to begin with. Similarly the Christian walk requires instruction, correction, change, and practice, as God is conforming each of us into the image of Christ. I pray that, as you read this book, you will be inspired by all that the Lord has given you to walk with Him by grace through faith.

Contents

Beyond the Dance

Strains of music faintly touch the silent figure resting in a halo of light. As though gently aroused through metamorphosis, she ascends as if out of a cocoon of dreams. Her arms float as she delicately but surely perches on a single point. Strength and beauty merge as she leaps and spins. With seemingly effortless grace she executes countless maneuvers as intricate as a tapestry of kaleidoscopic twists and turns held by threads of sustained extension.

The ballerina has not attained this state of perfection easily or magically. Her artistic development did not occur in a cocoon of sleep or dreams, but rather through years of rigorous training and practice.

In like manner, the woman of grace who belongs to the Lord moves confidently through life, expressing consistent love in words and actions emanating from a deep abiding presence of the Lord Jesus Christ. Peace flows through her words and actions because she has placed her trust in Jesus and continues to walk in faith. No matter what circumstances beset her, she finds the resources for love, joy, peace, patience, gentleness, goodness, faith, meekness, and self-control.

God's woman of grace came into this life-giving relationship with Him at a moment in time when by faith she received spiritual birth. Her transformation has continued through moment by moment choices to live according to this divine relationship. Each time she has chosen God's will above her own, she has developed more and more confidence in God. She lives by His life, by His Holy Spirit. She mounts up with wings as an eagle because she has learned to wait on God and to do His will.

To dance is to become one with the music—to feel the tones and cadences flow through arms and legs just as the bow is drawn across violin strings. Dance was a part of me throughout my early years. When I began to study ballet, I learned that the necessary freedom of expression, the grace and the strength, could be attained only through discipline and hard work. Every movement which enchants an audience has been preceded by thousands upon thousands of *pliés* and *tendus*, as well as many other exercises that tax the body to its limit. Yet an all-consuming love for ballet can make the hard work seem like nothing in comparison to the joy of dancing.

Throughout my teenage years I took as many ballet classes as I could and dreamed of dancing with a ballet company Then another love came into my life. His name is Martin, and he was also a dancer. We met at the ballet *barre*, continued studying ballet together, and danced professionally for awhile. However, because we had academic interests, we also attended the university. Then, as we started to raise a family, the ballet slippers, leotards, and tights were tucked away in boxes.

At various times I considered going back to ballet classes, but pride held me back. I knew that I had lost most of what I had gained through the many years of concentrated study. It would be like starting all over from the beginning. Then one day over 20 years away from the ballet *barre*, I returned. The first class was very basic. Although I was not starting at the very beginning, I had much to relearn. What had formerly become almost automatic was now accomplished only by concentrated effort. On the one hand I was delighted with what was being reawakened in me after lying dormant for so long. On the other hand, I was acutely aware of my lack of strength, endurance, and precision.

The major struggle initially was in regaining the stance and strength of correct body placement, which involves much more than standing up straight. During every movement at the *barre* I had to concentrate on both the movement itself and the body placement. And, as one adult beginner complained, "There are just too many things to think about all at the same time." However, the body placement and movements did come back more quickly than if I had not had extensive training previously. Then came the necessity to redevelop strength, control, and grace.

As I was relearning what had formerly become habit, I realized more than ever the parallels between the making of a dancer and the developing of a mature Christian. The parallels began to emerge: from the love of dance to the all-consuming love for Jesus; from the need for correct body placement to the need to be fully centered in Jesus; from the unending repetition of exercises to the daily choices to do things God's way; from the balance of discipline and freedom in ballet to the truth which sets Christians free to obey God; and from the dance as communication and expression to the life of Jesus being communicated and expressed outward to other people.

I thought of the grace of a dancer in relation to the gracious walk of a godly woman. The more proficient and experienced a dancer is, the less she appears to be working. Effort has been replaced by apparent ease. Strain has been replaced by grace. And the awkward stages of learning the most difficult steps have given way to a beauty which is both controlled and free. The same is true of a Christian woman who has learned to walk according to the Spirit. The more she has chosen to think and act according to God's design, the less she appears to be trying to be spiritual. She has given up on self-effort and has taken Jesus' yoke upon herself. The strain of sin and guilt has been replaced by forgiveness and grace. And as she has developed the habit of trusting and obeying God in a love relationship with Him, she walks in beauty which is both controlled and free.

Dancers spend hours at the *barre* and hours in the center, practicing and perfecting their skill. The same should be true of every Christian woman. No matter how long she has walked with God, she also continues in His training, ever seeking to do His will in countless situations. This book is for every woman who desires to walk with God and to continue growing more like Jesus every day.

1

Beginning Barre Work: Honoring and Thanking God

Easels, stacked-up canvases, the smell of paint and turpentine—all evoke a pang of nostalgia to those who have studied art. Such ordinary equipment signifies creativity, beauty, and effort. Likewise, the wooden *barres* and mirrors lining a ballet studio quicken my senses. I automatically readjust my posture and for a moment return to those days of exhilaration and hard work.

The ballet class begins at the *barre* (pronounced "bar"), which is a horizontal wooden pole bracketed to the wall at about waist height. The *barre* is the place of disciplined instruction and rigorous training. *Barre* exercises are composed of both isolated and combined elements of the dance. Each exercise is precise. There is a correct way to execute each movement and numerous possibilities for missing the mark. The freedom and apparent ease of an accomplished dancer come from the discipline at the *barre*.

A beginner learns the basic movements at the *barre*. As she progresses, she develops the ability to perform each movement with greater and greater strength and agility. The tempo may be increased or decreased. The instructor will vary the positions, repetitions, and variations of combinations with other movements in intermediate and advanced classes. The *barre* is not simply a warm-up place; it is a place of such disciplined instruction that the student must be constantly alert. *Barre* work prepares the dancer for physical accuracy, mental acuity and aesthetic sensibility

We may enjoy watching the exquisite precision and grace of a ballerina, but we rarely think of the rigors of the *barre* and the countless repetitions of both simple and complex movements. Likewise, when we observe a graceful woman of God who bears the fruit of the Spirit, we forget the many times she has chosen God's will over having her own way and how she has thereby developed godly habits of love. Both the ballerina and the Christian woman have developed through many repetitions, through many small steps. Ballet training reminds me of the absolute necessity of a disciplined life. However, for the Christian the discipline is an inner work as well as an outward obedience. Paul describes this discipline as "the mind set on the Spirit" (Romans 8:6).

Day after day, month after month, year after year, the dancers repeat the same exercises. One is the *plié* (pronounced "plee-AY"). It is of primary importance because it is performed in conjunction with nearly every other step. Beginners learn to plié during their first class. Advanced students and professional dancers continue the plié with greater precision and in various combinations of steps. *Pliés* are executed in the five ballet positions with the legs turned outward from the hips. The *demi* (or half) *plié* is done by bending the knees over the toes while keeping the heels on the floor and holding the body erect. The *plié* is then completed by returning to the original position. It is the solid position from which and to which many steps are made. All jumps must begin and end in the *plié*.

I see the *plié* as being symbolic of every Christian thought and activity proceeding from the desire to honor God and ending in giving Him thanks. Paul recognized the importance of honoring God and giving thanks. Romans chapter 1 includes very serious warnings concerning the neglect of honoring and thanking God:

> Even though they knew God, they did not honor Him as God, or give thanks; but they became futile in their speculations, and their foolish heart was darkened. Professing to be wise, they became fools.... Therefore God gave them over in the lusts of their hearts to impurity, that their bodies might be dishonored among them. For they exchanged the truth of God for a lie, and worshiped and served the creature rather than the Creator, who is blessed forever. Amen (Romans 1:21-25).

Honoring God as God and thanking Him are basic to the Christian walk. Whenever we choose our own way rather than God's way, we actually set ourselves up as little gods and "serve the creature (ourselves) rather than the Creator." However brief this may be, however subtle and unnoticed, even temporary self- enthroned godhood is dangerous to our spiritual well-being. Furthermore, when we fail to thank God, we may fail to remember that all good comes from Him.

The world does not honor God or thank Him. The world is involved in futile speculation and deception. The pull of the world, the pull of the flesh, and the pull of the devil can drag us down if we are not careful, alert, and diligent in honoring God and being grateful to Him.

Honoring God as God

When we acknowledge God as God and submit our lives to Him in every detail, we are honoring Him as God. When we believe His Word and trust Him in all circumstances, we are honoring Him as God. When we obey Him, we are honoring Him as God. We hold Him in reverence with such awe that we fear displeasing Him. This is not only because we may fear the consequences, but also because God is too wonderful and awesome to disobey. The wisdom of Proverbs calls this "the fear of the Lord," and says, "The fear of the Lord is the beginning of knowledge" (Proverbs 1:7).

Honoring God sounds well and good when He appears to be answering our prayers in the way we want Him to and when His will seems to coincide with our own. But how about the times when He works within our circumstances in such a way that things do not seem to be going our way? Remember Moses' sister Miriam? The time came in the wilderness when things were certainly not going her way. Wasn't she the one who had helped her mother carefully place baby Moses in his basket among the reeds? Wasn't she the one who hid herself and waited to see the fate of her baby brother? Wasn't she the one who listened as the Pharaoh's daughter decided to adopt Moses? Wasn't she the one God used to arrange for Moses to be nursed and raised by his own natural mother at the household expense of the Pharaoh? Why then didn't she have a share in the power?

Evidently Miriam was not content with the great privilege of serving God as a prophetess and worship leader. She wasn't satisfied with what God had chosen for her, and she began to honor herself more than God. Her own self-will got in the way of following the will of God. She and her brother Aaron began to murmur about Moses. They talked behind his back and said, "Has the Lord indeed spoken only through Moses? Has He not spoken through us as well?" (Numbers 12:2). In pride and self-will Miriam and Aaron grasped for position, but the Bible says of Moses, "Now the man Moses was very humble, more than any man who was on the face of the earth" (Numbers 12:3).

The Lord God, who hears the secret intents of the heart, rebuked Miriam and Aaron. When the cloud of His presence lifted, Miriam was leprous. In shock and grief Aaron knew that Miriam bore the punishment for his rebellion as well as for her own. He begged Moses to seek God on her account. "And Moses cried out to the Lord, saying, 'O God, heal her, I pray!'" Miriam bore her shame for seven days and then the Lord healed her. She had to learn the hard way that God is God—that He is the One who is in charge. He has the power and He has the responsibility. She also learned something about His love for her through His forgiveness and restoration. She turned from her own self-will to honor God as God in her life.

We often think of *fear* and *trust* as being contradictory terms. And indeed they are in most instances. However, when we fear God in a truly biblical sense, we also trust Him. Miriam neither feared nor trusted God when she chose to rebel against Him. However, when she began to honor Him as God, she once again feared and trusted Him. The only person we can both fear and trust is the One who loves us enough to keep us on the right path. We honor God by fearing and trusting Him.

Honoring God involves acknowledging Him in all that we do:

> Trust in the Lord with all your heart, And do not lean on your own understanding. In all your ways acknowledge Him, And He will make your paths straight (Proverbs 3:5, 6).

I have been jolted by that verse just when I am doing something that contradicts the very idea of acknowledging God. When I step on the gas pedal to zip around a poky driver to show him a thing or two, I am not acknowledging God. I must admit that I am still a student who needs to learn to honor God in all circumstances and in all places. I need to acknowledge Him while I am driving as well as when I am reading the Bible.

When we were children we used to see how long we could hold our breath. Then in the ballet class we tried to see how long we could balance in various difficult positions. Have you ever checked to see how long you have been able to maintain the position of acknowledging God in all you are doing? That is indeed a habit to work on! Just as a dancer needs to continue to practice her *pliés*, even when she has become a prima ballerina, every Christian woman will continue to practice honoring God in all she does. She will acknowledge Him in all her ways.

Gratitude

One exercise that should naturally follow the marvelous gift of life and salvation from sin and death is that of thanksgiving. Thankfulness should be our natural response to God. However, gratitude must be practiced in order to become a habitual state of mind. When we turn our eyes away from the goodness of God, we can easily fall into a habitual state of ingratitude. Miriam had allowed herself to complain. She had stopped thanking and praising God when she and Aaron joined in their rebellion. Ungratefulness is often the state of mind just before a person rebels against God and indulges in sin. Unless we choose to center our thoughts on His goodness to us, we put ourselves onto a path of dissatisfaction and destruction.

After God delivered the Israelites from the Egyptians through His dramatic intervention, the Israelites were full of praise and adoration. However, a few days later they were thirsty and began to complain bitterly against Moses and against God. Not only had they forgotten God's tremendous miracle of salvation, but they whined that they had been better off in Egypt! The Israelites were like one giant yo-yo. When circumstances were great they thanked God, but when the testing came they complained with ungrateful hearts. They had not developed a grateful attitude.

Gratitude may not come easily as a habit of mind. Too often a surge of thankfulness comes only in response to external happenings. Rather than simply being grateful when some terrific event occurs or some extravagant gift has been given, a woman of grace learns to cultivate gratitude as a manner of thinking, as an attitude of the heart. This exercise, therefore, may be practiced regardless of circumstances.

> Rejoice always; pray without ceasing; in everything give thanks; for this is God's will for you in Christ Jesus (1 Thessalonians 5:16-18).

> ...always giving thanks for all things in the name of our Lord Jesus Christ to God, even the Father (Ephesians 5:20).

Gratitude is the perfect condition of the heart for every moment of the day; it is a choice rather than simply a feeling that comes and goes. At the end of a particular Sunday evening service our pastor asked us to come forward and to just praise and thank God for His goodness to us. I was tired and did not feel like praising. I did not feel grateful. However, I went forward and explained to God that even though I did not feel grateful I did want to thank Him. As I began to thank Him silently in my heart by choice, I began to feel thankful. The choice to thank God released the feeling of gratitude; it began to trickle and then proceeded to flow throughout my entire being. I worshiped the Lord not because I felt like it but because I chose to obey Him. Worshipful feelings followed, but they are not essential for pleasing God.

> Enter His gates with thanksgiving,
> And His courts with praise.

Give thanks to Him; bless His name.
For the Lord is good;
His lovingkindness is everlasting,
And His faithfulness to all generations
(Psalm 100:4, 5).

Beginning the day with praise is God's way for us.

It is good to give thanks to the Lord,
And to sing praises to Thy name, O Most High;
To declare Thy lovingkindness in the morning,
And Thy faithfulness by night. . . .
For Thou, O Lord, hast made me glad by what
Thou has done;
I will sing for joy at the works of Thy hands
(Psalm 92:1, 2, 4).

God knows how much we need to exercise gratitude, not for His sake but for ours. Gratitude is so very important to our spiritual well-being that the apostle Paul lists ungratefulness as one of the characteristics of people who eventually enter into spiritual blindness, idolatry, impurity, and the vilest of passions and sin.

On the other hand, the benefits of gratitude far exceed what we might expect. For example, a thankful heart leads to love, joy peace, and other fruit of the Spirit. Gratitude moves in the opposite direction from self-pity, dissatisfaction, jealousy, and depression, because the gaze is fixed upon God and His goodness rather than upon the circumstances around us.

A ballet dancer would be foolish if she thought she could perfect and retain a particular step after only practicing it a short time. On the other hand, Christians often think that there should be immediate success in changing behavior and developing godly habits. But we do not change easily, even with the enabling of the Lord. That is why we must continually practice honoring God and thanking Him.

Honoring and thanking God is quite an assignment if it is to be practiced daily. If you choose to be diligent in this first exercise "at the *barre*," you will find that your Teacher will begin to correct you so that you will become more and more adept at honoring and thanking God. The Holy Spirit is faithful to discipline us as we choose to discipline ourselves. He will gently but firmly press the knee so that it is directly over the foot during the *plié*; that is, He will gently but firmly help us to honor and thank the Father with consistency.

Devotional Exercise

1. Read Matthew 5:3-16. Write down ways that you can honor God in your own circumstances.

2. Purpose to honor God in your attitudes, thoughts, words, and actions. Ask the Holy Spirit to nudge you when you are not honoring Him as you have purposed in your heart. Look to Him to enable you to turn again to honor God.

3. Write the Lord a thank-you letter.

2

Position: Christ-Centered

We walked away from the ballet *barre* and took our positions for the center work. The instructor demonstrated a combination of adagio movements and the music began. We began with a series of slow transitions from one position of difficult balance to another, with one leg lifted and being extended in various directions. Between transitions, we raised up onto *demi-point* for even more difficult balancing. Some dancers wiggled around to accommodate the shifting of weight. Others kept the extended leg low, just in case they were to lose their balance. Others had to interrupt the sequence to regain balance. But the dancers who had learned to center their bodies with each change in movement were able to execute every transition with apparent ease.

Because security is an absolute necessity for a dancer, she must develop correct body placement. From a secure center of balance and control, she may progressively learn more difficult movements. To establish and maintain proper placement, she centers her weight over her supporting foot. At the same time she pulls up around her center point of balance so that she is neither drooping nor overcompensating. Because many of the steps she will be performing are swift, she must be able to readjust her weight quickly to keep her balance.

Every pirouette, leap, arabesque, and step are dependent upon the accuracy of body placement. Even the slightest degree of misplacement may hinder the performance of multiple turns. Accurate centering gives control and grace to each movement. It is also essential for preventing injuries.

Just as a dancer gains physical security through correct body placement, a Christian woman gains her sense of security through developing the habit of centering in Christ. As her faith is securely placed in Jesus, she has inner security and strength to perform what is right and good even in the midst of turmoil and stress. When she is rightly centered in Him, she can stand strong and tall because she is standing in His love and righteousness.

When a dancer-to-be enters her first ballet class, she enters a new world. As a girl or woman enters into new life through faith in Jesus, she becomes born again through receiving God's forgiveness and His indwelling Holy Spirit. She becomes a new creature ready to learn and perform the will of God. Jesus places us in Himself when we confess our sins and believe that He died to pay the penalty for our sins. He comes into our lives when we believe in Him and ask Him to be our Savior and Lord. We then learn to center our lives in Him by faith. Jesus accomplishes the primary work of placing us in Himself through His death and resurrection. He also comes to live in us to enable us to center our lives in Him.

Centering in Jesus is living in the midst of His love. This means believing His love and His Word even when every circumstance and feeling may deny that very love. The apostle Paul understood the importance of this love relationship, and he prayed for believers that God—

> ...would grant you, according to the riches of His glory, to be strengthened with power through His Spirit in the inner man; so that Christ may dwell in your hearts through faith; and that you, being rooted and grounded in love, may be able to comprehend with all the saints what is the breadth and length and height and depth, and to know the love of Christ, which surpasses knowledge, that you may be filled up to all the fulness of God (Ephesians 3:16-19).

Being centered in Christ is living in a love relationship with Him in which we receive and believe His love, and by which we in turn love Him through obedience. Jesus described this centering in Him through the analogy of the vine and the branches.

> Abide in Me, and I in you. As the branch cannot bear fruit of itself, unless it abides in the vine, so neither can you, unless you abide in Me. I am the vine, you are the branches; he who abides in Me, and I in him, he bears much fruit; for apart from Me you can do nothing (John 15:4, 5).

Everything a Christian does must proceed from this place of living in Jesus.

A number of years ago I was studying that portion of Scripture, and I thought I had come to an understanding of abiding. I felt Jesus' presence. I felt His love. We can feel wonderful when there are no pressures around us and we are completely alone with God. For instance, I find that I have wonderful patience when patience is not needed. I have great peace when circumstances are easy. I can feel wonderful goodness when I am just sitting alone with God and thinking. I had been experiencing all of these lovely feelings, but then I had to go into the kitchen to prepare food for my family.

I continued sensing the Lord's presence and with it the sense of love, joy, and peace. But then the children started acting up. I could feel tension coming in, and I began to lose my sense of abiding. Then I became furious with the children. They had ruined the abiding, or at least what I had mistakenly thought to be abiding. Later that day I recognized my mistake. I was thinking that abiding necessitates certain wonderful feelings. Yet Jesus wanted me to know that abiding is not just a sense but a reality. He wanted me to know that He was truly there with me in the kitchen to enable me to have His patience when I needed it and His peace in the midst of strife. Abiding goes beyond the prayer closet; abiding in Jesus is essential in the battles of life!

For a dancer, correct body placement is not an end in itself; it enables her to dance. Likewise for a believer, abiding is not just for the good feelings and the sense of security. Abiding is for living, for bearing fruit. And even though we may enjoy the fruit of the Spirit in our own lives, that fruit is for greater purposes than just our own enjoyment: The fruit is to glorify God and benefit His kingdom.

Fruit comes when we are trusting Jesus in whatever activities or circumstances come our way. The oneness and confident trust in Him enable us to represent our Lord in every situation. Before coming into relationship with Jesus through salvation, we trusted in our own selves to think and do what we wanted to do. But we were limited. Some of us may have lacked confidence to do mighty feats. Others of us had more self-confidence than our abilities warranted. However, when our faith and trust are in Jesus, He fills us so that the fruit of the Spirit becomes evident in our lives.

Abiding in Jesus is living His way by His grace for His purposes. That is why He said:

> If you abide in Me, and My words abide in you, ask whatever you wish, and it shall be done for you. By this is My Father glorified, that you bear much fruit, and so prove to be My disciples (John 15:7, 8).

The oneness of desiring the same things that God purposes is basic to abiding in Jesus. Communication with Him is possible at any hour to discuss every situation and to "find grace to help in time of need" (Hebrews 4:16).

Abiding in Jesus is living by His love, which surpasses our human understanding. In fact, to consider that Jesus loves us "just as" the Father loves Him is more than we can possibly grasp. Nevertheless Jesus said:

Just as the Father has loved Me, I have also loved you; abide in My love. If you keep My commandments you will abide in My love, just as I have kept My Father's commandments and abide in His love (John 15:9, 10).

Living by the love of Jesus is a two-way relationship. He loves us to the point of having given His life. We express our love for Him by keeping His commandments. In other words, obedience is a very fundamental way of loving God. Jesus is not saying that He will love us only if we obey Him; He is encouraging the full relationship of both receiving and giving love. Although many feelings may accompany love, our love relationship with Jesus is neither dependent upon feelings nor measured by them.

Feelings are not reliable indicators of how much we may be loving Jesus at the moment, although there are certain attitudes which accompany this love relationship. One primary attitude is that of joy. Jesus declared, "These things I have spoken to you that My joy may be in you and that your joy may be made full" (John 15:11). This attitude of joy cannot be dependent upon circumstances, nor can it be measured by superficial feelings. Joy is related to love and trust. Jesus had this kind of joy even while hanging on the cross. The writer to the Hebrews described Jesus as the "author and perfecter of faith, who for the joy set before Him endured the cross, despising the shame, and has sat down at the right hand of the throne of God" (Hebrews 12:2).

Abiding in Jesus branches out into loving one another:

> This is My commandment, that you love one
> another, just as I have loved you. Greater love
> has no one than this, that one lay down his life for
> his friends. You are my friends if you do what I
> command you. No longer do I call you slaves, for
> the slave does not know what his master is doing;
> but I have called you friends, for all things that I
> have heard from My Father I have made known
> to you. You did not choose Me, but I chose you,
> and appointed you, that you should go and bear
> fruit, and that your fruit should remain, that
> whatever you ask of the Father in My name, He
> may give to you. This I command you, that you
> love one another (John 15:12-17).

The more we love each other, the more intimate our relation ship is with Jesus. And the more we center our lives in Him, the more we will love one another.

A woman especially needs Jesus' love because she has been created for relationship. Relationships with people may not supply the love she desires, and at times she may be giving out more love than she is receiving from other people. But Jesus' love is always there to strengthen and restore.

Being centered in Christ is to be loved and to love. One woman responded to Jesus' love by washing His feet with perfume and tears.

> There was a woman in the city who was a sinner;
> and when she learned that He was reclining at
> the table in the Pharisee's house, she brought an
> alabaster vial of perfume, and standing behind
> Him at His feet, weeping, she began to wet His

feet with her tears, and kept wiping them with the hair of her head, and kissing His feet, and anointing them with the perfume (Luke 7:37, 38).

The Pharisee had critical thoughts toward the woman, and so Jesus told him the parable of two debtors. One owed a great deal of money and the other only a small amount. Jesus asked the Pharisee which debtor was more grateful when his debt had been canceled. The Pharisee answered, "I suppose the one whom he forgave more" (Luke 7:43). Then Jesus applied the parable to the woman and the Pharisee, who had not even arranged for Jesus to wash His own feet after traveling on the dusty road. In contrast, the woman had been lavishly ministering to His needs with perfume and tears. Then Jesus explained why: She had responded to His love and forgiveness.

> For this reason I say to you, her sins, which are many, have been forgiven, for she loved much; but he who is forgiven little loves little (Luke 7:47).

Jesus then reaffirmed that her sins were forgiven and said to her, "Your faith has saved you; go in peace" (Luke 7:50).

Jesus' love is received through faith. Sometimes feelings accompany His love, but not always. Sometimes circumstances confirm His love, but many times they do not. To center one's life in Jesus is to believe that He loves us, no matter what. However, receiving love is still only half the story. The woman who anointed Jesus with perfume and tears received His love by faith, but she also loved Jesus through what she chose to do. She loved Him in her heart and mind, and she expressed her love through action.

Because proper centering is so important in ballet, large mirrors line the walls of ballet studios. Dancers regularly check their body placement with the help of mirrors. Even though a dancer may think she is correctly placed because she feels balanced, she may not be accurately centered. She may be straining certain muscles to compensate for the lack of proper positioning. For the dancer, the mirror reveals an element of truth, indicating whether or not she is properly centered and executing a step correctly. When she glances into the mirror, it is not to admire her own beauty or how wonderfully well she is performing. Rather, she checks to see if change or adjustment is necessary.

The Christian woman has two mirrors by which she may check her centering in Christ. The first is Jesus Himself.

> We all, with unveiled face beholding as in a mirror the glory of the Lord, are being transformed into the same image from glory to glory just as from the Lord, the Spirit (2 Corinthians 3:18).

As we look at the love and character of Jesus, who lives in us and in whom we desire to center our lives, we become more like Him and even begin to reflect Him. We can check whether or not we are centered in Him by checking our actions with how He would act. We can compare our words with His words. We can even monitor our thoughts with what we know about His thoughts. God has also given us another mirror, and that is His Word, the Bible. James wrote about this mirror:

> Prove yourselves doers of the word, and not merely hearers who delude themselves. For if anyone is a hearer of the word and not a doer, he is like a man who looks at his natural face in a mirror; for once he has looked at himself and gone away he has immediately forgotten what kind of person he was. But one who looks intently at the perfect law, the law of liberty, and abides by it, not having become a forgetful hearer but an effectual doer, this man shall be blessed in what he does (James 1:22-25).

Centering in Christ involves both faith and action. When we look into the Word of God, we can see whether we are correctly centered in Jesus and whether we are walking according to the life and love of Christ. The Word teaches what is right and also indicates error. It gives necessary information concerning correction:

> All Scripture is inspired by God and profitable for teaching, for reproof, for correction, for training in righteousness; that the man of God may be adequate, equipped for every good work (2 Timothy 3:16-17).

One ballet teacher suggested that students stand in front of a mirror the first thing in the morning. They were to place themselves in correct alignment and then attempt to maintain the posture throughout the day. We too can look into the mirror of the Word of God, find our correct spiritual placement in Jesus, and then remember to place our faith and trust in Him throughout the day.

Devotional Exercise

1. Read John 3:16; Romans 3:23; Romans 6:23; Romans 10:9, 10; and Ephesians 2:8, 9. Have you received salvation through faith in Jesus? If you do not have an assurance of salvation, confess that you are a sinner. Ask Jesus to forgive you and to give you His life. Thank Him for dying in your place to accomplish your salvation. Purpose to follow Him as Lord of your life.

2. Read Ephesians 3:16-19 and pray this prayer for three other people and for yourself each day for one week.

3. Read John 15 every day for a week and practice living in Jesus in everything you do or say. Jot down words and actions that fit into abiding in Jesus. Also jot down those that don't fit and that you would like to change.

3

The Perfect Combination: The Gifts, The Word, The Woman

Martin and I sat in the third row. A small company from Europe had come to Santa Barbara to perform a ballet version of Anton Chekov's *Three Sisters*. As the curtain opened, the three sisters posed as still life around a tree while a soprano entered from the back of the auditorium. Her wordless voice sang the longing of the sisters' hearts. As the three sisters began to dance, their expertise marked them as seasoned, professional dancers. Each danced a different character with grace, agility, and artistic expression. Each movement was precise, yet graceful—perfect, yet unpretentious.

I have attended student performances in the same auditorium, and even from the balcony my ears have heard the clunking of the blocked toe shoes. And yet, even during leaps and intricate point work, the ballerinas of this professional company made hardly a sound. There was only a soft swishing on the floor. They had so perfected their art as to enchant the audience with virtuoso and delicacy.

Ballet is a much more demanding art than one might imagine. Hopes are high and intentions are good when girls begin to study ballet, but few continue into excellence. Most remain at some stage of mediocrity or eventually drop out because progress is slow and so much work is involved. Many Christians begin their new walk with high hopes and zeal, but often they too reach a plateau, relinquish their first love, and settle for less than God intends. What makes the difference? How does a dancer attain artistic excellence and how does a Christian attain excellence in her spiritual walk with the Lord? How does she reflect the image of Jesus in the fullness of His character?

For a dancer to become a sensitive and skilled artist, she must have both natural talent and the right physical makeup. Without natural talent, she may have the best training and may work very hard, but she will always be limited. On the other hand, a perfect body, great natural talent, and excellent teaching will all go to waste if the dancer does not do her part. She must bring her entire being under discipline. The delicate-looking ballerina daily pours forth all of herself at peak energy outlay Her incredible power and grace develop only after years of training that exceed even the rigorous requirements of many athletes.

The *quality* of training also makes a great difference, because without excellent teaching a dancer may develop numerous bad habits and even physical problems, which could prevent her from performing difficult steps. For a dancer to develop into an outstanding performing artist, she must have both natural gifts and excellent training. And she must also be willing to put forth astounding effort.

The Gifts

Natural talent and the physical build of a dancer are innate gifts which cannot be earned. Every Christian woman has unearned gifts that she has received from the hand of her Creator and Savior. He has given her the gift of salvation:

> By grace you have been saved through faith; and that not of yourselves, it is the gift of God; not as a result of works, that no one should boast. For we are His workmanship, created in Christ Jesus for good works, which God prepared before- hand, that we should walk in them (Ephesians 2:8-10).

Salvation is a gift that brings with it a number of other gifts. The gift includes new life in Jesus which is eternal:

> The wages of sin is death, but the free gift of God is eternal life in Christ Jesus our Lord (Romans 6:23).

Every person who repents of sin and trusts Jesus for salvation receives forgiveness from sin and the gift of the Holy Spirit. When the crowd heard Peter's sermon on the day of Pentecost, they were "pierced to the heart" and asked Peter what they could do: "Peter said to them, 'Repent, and let each of you be baptized in the name of

Jesus Christ for the forgiveness of your sins; and you shall receive the gift of the Holy Spirit'" (Acts 2:38).

Jesus explained to the disciples that He would send the Holy Spirit to live in them.

> I will ask the Father, and He will give you another Helper, that He may be with you forever; that is the Spirit of truth, whom the world cannot receive, because it does not behold Him or know Him, but you know Him because He abides with you, and will be in you (John 14:16,17).

The Holy Spirit is a marvelous gift, superior to every natural talent on earth. Each believer receives the Holy Spirit to live in her. He guides her into truth. He helps her understand and apply God's Word in daily living. He encourages her in the ways of God and enables her to live in purity and holiness.

> The Helper, the Holy Spirit, whom the Father will send in My name, He will teach you all things, and bring to your remembrance all that I said to you (John 14:26).

> When He, the Spirit of truth, comes, He will guide you into all the truth; for He will not speak on His own initiative, but whatever He hears, He will speak; and He will disclose to you what is to come. He shall glorify Me; for He shall take of Mine and shall disclose it to you (John 16:13, 14).

The Holy Spirit gives power to live according to God's truth and grace. Gifts are very exciting for children, and the anticipation is sometimes almost too much to bear.

How well I remember my tenth Christmas! The presents from out-of-town relatives had arrived a couple of weeks before, and my mother had hidden them in an old bassinet in the hallway just outside my room. One day I could bear the suspense no longer. I quietly lifted the cover and examined the presents. Nearly every gift had a tag, but the ones from my grandmother didn't. With unrestrained curiosity I carefully unwrapped the ends and quickly discovered which ones were for my father and brother. However, I had to open the two other gifts to get a better look. One was a nail kit with nail polish, nail file, and emery boards. The other was an exquisite set of eight tiny silver salt-and-pepper shakers. Since I had not yet developed an interest in keeping my nails filed or using nail polish, I was sure that the nail kit was for my mother. That left the cunning little salt-and-pepper shakers for me, or at least that was what I thought. Having peeked at the gifts made me even more eager for Christmas Eve to arrive. I could hardly wait to open the special package from Grandma.

When Christmas Eve finally came, there was some discussion about Grandma's undesignated gifts. We each opened one and held it up. The one for my brother was obviously for him, since no one else was interested in a toy truck. My mother was delighted with the miniature salt-and-pepper shakers and declared that they were exactly what she had wanted. And then she expressed her enthusiastic approval over what Grandma had chosen for me—the nail kit. My disappointment was so great that I could not take pleasure in the gift which was truly more appropriate for me. After all, what would a ten-year-old do with salt-and-pepper shakers?

I could not appreciate the gift that had been chosen for me because I had expected something else. That can happen to all of us when it comes to gifts from God. Just because we do not have the gift of some natural talent which we have coveted, we do not fully value the spiritual gift of the indwelling Holy Spirit.

The Holy Spirit lives in us to glorify the Father and to bring forth fruit. Thus each of us has been endowed with a gift that has greater possibilities than we have yet discovered. Without the Holy Spirit, we could have the best teachers and we could work extremely hard, but we would not produce fruit or glorify God. Many people who have learned and followed some of the principles of God's Word may look and act very much like Christians. However, without His life inside them, they are like the most beautifully crafted artificial fruit. They look like the real thing, but provide no nourishment or seed.

The Word

In addition to having the gifts of talent and the right physical makeup, the dancer must have accurate and inspiring instruction. As Christians, we have been given gifts, but we also need instruction. The Holy Spirit is active in this part of our spiritual growth. He teaches and guides us into all truth. Furthermore, we have the written Word of God. Peter recognized that we indeed have been given all that we need for life and godliness. He began his second letter this way:

> Grace and peace be multiplied to you in the
> knowledge of God and of Jesus our Lord; seeing
> that His divine power has granted to us everything
> pertaining to life and godliness, through the true
> knowledge of Him who called us by His own glory
> and excellence. For by these He has granted to us
> His precious and magnificent promises, in order
> that by them you might become partakers of the
> divine nature, having escaped the corruption that
> is in the world by lust (2 Peter 1:2-4).

We can read the Bible for ourselves, and we have the
Spirit of truth resident within us to help us understand
and apply the truth. He is indeed our primary teacher.

Many people have expressed to me how the Word
of God made sense to them only after they became
Christians. Without the Holy Spirit, a person could
devote his life to teaching "The Bible As Literature."
With an unredeemed mind, he may scorn the very book
he is teaching. A professor at one of the universities
which I attended had the reputation of tossing the Bible
onto the floor and standing on it to demonstrate his belief
that the Bible was just an ordinary book with no divine
authorship or authority. He had not had the right Tutor.
Of course the Bible is printed on ordinary paper, but the
contents are the revealed and recorded Word of God.

God has also given to the church people who are
especially gifted and prepared to instruct and equip
believers to serve God and to build up the body of Christ.

> He gave some as apostles, and some as prophets,
> and some as evangelists, and some as pastors and
> teachers, for the equipping of the saints for the

work of service, to the building up of the body of Christ; until we all attain to the unity of the faith, and of the knowledge of the Son of God, to a mature man, to a measure of the stature which belongs to the fulness of Christ (Ephesians 4:11-13).

We need accurate instruction in the Word of God. Because we have the Holy Spirit and because we are able to read the Word for ourselves, we should be able to discern whether a person is a good teacher or not. Furthermore, we can discover whether a person is a good teacher by looking at his or her life. The teacher should be consistent with the teaching. Paul was able to say, "The things you have learned and received and heard and seen in me, practice these things; and the God of peace shall be with you" (Philippians 4:9).

As you and I walk with the Lord in obedience by faith, and as we read and study the Bible, we will know the way of the Lord. Personal study of the Word is essential for every believer.

The Woman

Just as a dancer must put forth great effort and must persevere through many classes and repetitions, so the Christian woman has a great responsibility about her own walk with the Lord. God has given His precious gifts of salvation, new life, and the indwelling Holy Spirit. He has provided His Word, and also people to teach by word and deed. He has called each of His daughters to walk with Him in a love relationship which surpasses any human companionship. As she responds to all that God has done for her, she will do all that He shows her to do.

After writing about God's provision of "everything pertaining to life and godliness," Peter challenged the Christians:

> For this very reason also, applying all diligence, in your faith supply moral excellence, and in your moral excellence, knowledge; and in your knowledge, self-control, and in your self-control, perseverance, and in your perseverance, godliness; and in your godliness, brotherly kindness, and in your brotherly kindness, love. For if these qualities are yours and are increasing, they render you neither useless nor unfruitful in the true knowledge of our Lord Jesus Christ (2 Peter 1:5-8).

Jesus equips us to do His will and to bear fruit, but He gives us opportunities to do our part. He involves us as participants in what He is doing. We then have the divine privilege of responding to His love through obedience and devotion.

The orange tree just outside my window is laden with both fruit and clusters of blossoms. The sun glistens on a simple spider web and transforms it into an ethereal piece of artistic splendor. The bees busily flit from blossom to blossom without distraction or wavering. God made the tree and provides for its nourishment and growth. He made the spider and the bee. He gifted them with skill to do the work that He designed for them. The tree, the spider, and the bee respond to His plan by working consistently to do their part in God's universe.

Just as God has placed the "knowledge" in the tree, spider, and bee so that they "know" what they are to do,

He instructs us and tells us what to do. The difference, however, lies in the fact that we choose whether or not we will obey God. And we have many subtle ways of escaping clear understanding of His will when we don't want to obey The tree, spider, and bee don't seem to have a real choice in the matter. Their natural instinct includes the law of God for them. But our part can only be accomplished through desiring to find out what God says and then doing it.

Jesus' first miracle is an excellent example of how God uses human involvement in accomplishing His will. Jesus, His mother, and His disciples were all guests at a wedding in Cana of Galilee. Suddenly the wine ran out. Mary turned to Jesus for help. She had such trust in her son that she proceeded to tell the servants to do whatever He said. Jesus instructed them to fill six huge stone waterpots with fresh water. The servants obeyed. They filled the pots to the brim.

Jesus' next instruction was rather unusual, since the waterpots were not customarily used for drinking water, but rather for ceremonial washing. Jesus asked the servants to draw out some water and take it to the headwaiter. They must have thought this rather foolish, but they obeyed. And they must have been quite surprised at the reaction of the headwaiter, for when he had sipped the water he was quite pleased. He exclaimed that this wine was far superior to the wine which had been served earlier.

Jesus performed the miracle of changing water into wine, but He asked for the cooperation of ordinary people. The servants obeyed Jesus even though they did not understand what He was really doing. On the one hand, the servants could have poured and served water all day and the water would not have turned into wine if Jesus had not performed the miracle. On the other hand, it is possible to wonder if Jesus would have chosen to complete this miracle without human involvement.

The woman who desires to grow in grace will do all she can to know and perform according to God's Word. She will be like the Thessalonians, whom Paul addressed this way:

> We give thanks to God always for all of you, making mention of you in our prayers; constantly bearing in mind your work of faith and labor of love and steadfastness of hope in our Lord Jesus Christ in the presence of our God and Father, knowing, brethren beloved by God, His choice of you (1 Thessalonians 1:2-4).

The loveliness of a woman who lives this way is that she reflects Jesus. She bears fruit where there is hunger. Living waters flow forth from her to quench the thirst of parched lives. She becomes more and more intimate in her relationship with her Lord and Savior.

Ballet classes are not for light amusement or personal entertainment; they require supreme effort. Dancers give great care to every movement. They expend every ounce of energy. Their breathing becomes audible, and faces are bathed in perspiration. As they repeat the same exercise over and over again, their concentration intensifies. They may not even notice a bleeding toe or a cramped muscle until the end of a set of exercises. A dancer cannot afford to be lazy. If she is, she develops all kinds of bad habits, which will eventually destroy her dancing.

Everything must be done accurately over and over again. The demands for precision and strength are relentless.

Likewise, a Christian woman cannot afford to be lazy in her walk with the Lord. Though she may rest in Him through faith, she will lose ground if she becomes sloppy in her walk with Him. She must take great care to glorify her Lord and Savior in all that she does. She must spend time with her Lord and learn His Word and His ways.

My first years of ballet training were quite excellent. However, when we moved to a different city, I had to change teachers. My new teacher had many students and was highly regarded. However, he was a poor teacher as far as monitoring body placement. With great drama he demonstrated the movements, but he did not watch over us. Several girls had knees go out, and there were a number of other unnecessary injuries. When I finally realized that I was actually deteriorating, I quickly looked for another teacher. At last I found one who was truly excellent, and he helped me recover the loss. I was so tremendously grateful that I could not thank him enough. However, one day he looked at me with his piercing eyes and said, "The teacher can only teach. It is the student who must learn."

Personal responsibility and self-discipline are important aspects of the Christian walk, but we are not alone. Jesus has called us to participate with Him. He is with us and in us, enabling us and loving us all the way. Although we are to be actively involved, we are not left to our own self-effort, since we live the new life in relationship with Jesus.

God has given the gift of His own Son, Jesus, to cancel our sins, and He has given us His righteousness in place of our old sinful condition. He has given us eternal life in Himself. He has given us His Holy Spirit to teach, guide, and enable us to glorify Him. He has given us His holy written Word. He has given teachers to equip us. And He has given us the privilege and the responsibility to do our part by cooperating with Him so that He might fulfill His good purposes in us and through us.

All exercises at the *barre* lead to the goal of theatrical performance. Yet the magnificent glory of a ballet performance pales in comparison to the wondrous glory of God, which can be revealed through a woman who has received His gift of life. The transformation from sinner to saint is grander than the metamorphosis of an awkward girl into a prima ballerina. We are humbled by the awesome call to glorify Him every day. What a privilege to belong to the Company of God!

Devotional Exercise

1. List the gifts which the Lord has given to you. Thank Him for these gifts and purpose to use these gifts to glorify Him.

2. Ask the Holy Spirit to teach you as you read 2 Peter 1:2-4. Write out what this Scripture says in your own words and what it means to you. How does it apply to your life right now?

3. Read 2 Peter 1:5-8. Which of these qualities do you desire to increase in your own life? Ask God which one you need to diligently apply to your life right now.

4

Garments: Old and New

All eyes focus on the ballerina as she takes her position center stage. She is wearing a glittering black tutu. Black feathers frame her face. She is Odile, the black swan in Swan Lake. Her magnificent costume and dramatic display of brilliant technique reveal to the audience her true identity. However, the prince, who has fallen in love with Odette, mistakenly believes that this beautiful woman dressed in black is simply a different enchantment of his beloved.

The prince is fooled because Odile looks just like Odette. And, as a matter of fact, the same ballerina dances both parts. Only the costume and style of dance reveal the true identity. The black swan is the evil sorcerer's daughter impersonating Odette. Although the prince is fooled, the audience is not. The audience depends upon the costume to reveal the character. No wonder Shakespeare penned the famous lines in Hamlet, "The

51

apparel oft proclaims the man." He also depended on costumes as well as script to identify characters.

As essential as it is for a dancer to wear the proper costume, it is even more important that a Christian woman wear her God-given spiritual attire. Paul used this analogy of clothing when he spoke of putting off the old self and putting on the new. After describing the condition of a person who has not received new life through salvation, Paul wrote that the believers should lay aside the old ways of living and begin living according to the new life.

> But you did not learn Christ in this way [the old way], if indeed you have heard Him and have been taught in Him, just as truth is in Jesus, that in reference to your former manner of life, you lay aside the old self, which is being corrupted in accordance with the lusts of deceit, and that you be renewed in the spirit of your mind, and put on the new self, which in the likeness of God has been created in righteousness and holiness of the truth (Ephesians 4:20-24).

There should be no contradiction between the inner life and the external manner of living. Donning spiritual attire is simply putting on all that Christ has already put within.

Costumes are usually supplied by the ballet company but it is up to the dancer to put them on. Likewise, a Christian woman is given spiritual attire when she believes in Jesus as Savior and Lord, but she must choose to put on her new wardrobe. She actually has a moment-by-moment choice to clothe herself with the habits and ways of her former unredeemed self or to clothe herself with new ways which are consistent with the life of the Holy Spirit living within her.

Spiritual garments are described in a number of ways in the New Testament. In the passage just quoted, the new garment is the "new self, which in the likeness of God has been created in righteousness and holiness of the truth." The new garments which Jesus provided through salvation resemble the very likeness of God.

When God created Adam and Eve, He created them in His likeness. God said, "Let Us make man in Our image, according to Our likeness. . . ." And God created man in His own image, in the image of God He created him; male and female He created them (Genesis 1:26,27).

However, this likeness became distorted when Adam and Eve chose to disobey God. Eve was deceived into thinking that she would gain more by eating the forbidden fruit than by obeying God, and she drew Adam into sinful rebellion. Consequently they both lost their garments: the likeness of God. When they realized they were naked, they attempted to cover their sin and nakedness with garments of fig leaves. Fig leaves represent all that we put on in attempting to cover our own sinfulness, such as excuses, blame, and self-justification, as well as self-righteousness in all its pride and false humility.

When God found Adam and Eve in the Garden, dressed in the clumsy contrivance of their own conniving, He confronted them with the truth of what they had done and what the consequences would be. However, He took pity on them and clothed them in the skins of animals which had to be slain. These skins represented the dire need for atonement for sin. They foreshadowed the garments of righteousness which only the blood of Jesus could ultimately provide.

When Jesus died on the cross for humanity, He opened the way for every believer to be clothed in His righteousness. Every Christian has the privilege of putting on the spiritual garment of righteousness and truth in the likeness of God. This garment is more than exterior clothing, however, because it matches the characteristics of the Holy Spirit dwelling inside. Furthermore, the garments have a reflective quality because they reflect the Lord Jesus Christ. And because the garments belong to Jesus, just as we belong to Jesus, they are also robes of relationship.

Jesus told a parable about a king who had made extensive preparations for his son's wedding. He had sent out the proper invitations and expected an enthusiastic response, for this was to be one of the most elaborate and glorious events of the year. When the day arrived, the king eagerly sent his servants to announce that the long-awaited event was at hand. He was utterly shocked and dismayed when his servants returned laden down with one excuse after another. The king was very angry. Can you imagine planning a gala event at great expense and having no one come? Well, that is exactly what happened. Only this was worse, because this was his son's wedding! To think that no one even cared enough to be there! Indeed, such people were not worthy to be at the wedding in the first place!

Well, the king was not about to have a private wedding—not in those days when a wedding was characterized by much feasting and rejoicing. Therefore he thought of a plan. He would provide guests for his son's wedding. He sent his servants out into the public areas, highways, and lanes—wherever they could find people who were willing to come to the wedding.

In those days it was not enough to simply agree to attend a wedding and to arrive. Preparations had to be made, because every invited guest was expected to wear a special garment—a wedding garment. It would be like a formal wedding today with all guests expected to wear formal attire. Those who did decide to attend the wedding had to come with appropriate clothing.

The servants were successful. They supplied an abundance of guests. However, when the king came in to greet the guests he found one man who did not have the decency to put on a wedding garment. The king asked him, "Friend, how did you come in here without wedding clothes?" The man had no answer to give the king and was cast out into the darkness. The proper clothing was essential, because in this parable the garment represented the righteousness of Christ. People cannot enter into the presence of God in their own vestments of self-righteousness; they must be robed in the righteousness of Christ.

The first group of invited guests who refused to attend the wedding represented those to whom the promises of God had been given, but refused to believe that Jesus was the Son of God, the Savior. The man who came to the wedding dressed in the wrong clothing represents those who want to come to God on the basis of their own worth and righteousness. The guests who arrived at the wedding feast properly attired represent those who recognize that they do not have righteousness in themselves. They recognize their need for a Savior.

God has provided appropriate clothing for every person who joins His kingdom by faith. The garment is that of love, truth, and righteousness. The apostle Paul went into detail concerning the old clothing to set aside and the new garments to put on:

> Do not lie to one another, since you laid aside the old self with its evil practices, and have put on the new self, who is being renewed to a true knowledge according to the image of the One who created him. . . . And so, as those who have been chosen of God, holy and beloved, put on a heart of compassion, kindness, humility, gentleness and patience; bearing with one another and forgiving each other, whoever has a complaint against anyone; just as the Lord forgave you, so also should you. And beyond all these things put on love, which is the perfect bond of unity (Colossians 3:9, 10, 12-14).

When we put on Christ, all the features listed by Paul are included in the garment. However, the list is extremely helpful, because if we find that we are not acting according to the description of His garment, we can quickly put off the old and put on the new.

During the busy weeks of shopping before Christmas, parking can be quite a problem. One day as I was seeking a precious spot I noticed that a woman was just putting her baby into the car seat and would surely be pulling out of her parking place soon. I pulled over a bit so that other cars could pass while I waited. Just as she began to pull out a man zipped around me and right into that spot for which I had been patiently waiting! At first I was stunned. I could hardly believe the outright rudeness. He had stolen my spot! Suddenly I was no longer wearing the garment of patience and tranquility. I was furious! But as I drove around some more looking for a spot, I considered what it would be like to live or work with a person like that. There was some consolation in the fact that I would probably never again encounter this man.

I would like to say that I immediately put aside all the mean thoughts I had about him. Even though it was a small thing compared to many circumstances which test us, I had to make a conscious choice to put on "a heart of compassion." This does not mean that we just let things happen when we put off the old self and put on the new. No, we are actually better equipped to change a situation when we put on the new self. Dressed in the garment of Christ's wisdom and character, we know what is worth changing and what we can do to help bring about change. The parking incident was not worth changing, and only Jesus can change a person. However, I could pray for the man, and that could be the beginning of change for him.

Putting off the old self may also imply putting aside certain habits by putting on new habits. Throughout my childhood I entertained myself with daydreaming between the time I had to go to bed and the time I finally fell asleep. These were not just passive daydreams; they were detailed stories about myself being a wonderful heroine who surpassed all kinds of obstacles and whom everyone admired. The details of these stories included word-for-word conversations, clothing, and interior design as well as complicated plot. Even though I did not listen to serials during those days of radio, one of my own stories with all its details would go on for weeks. Every night I had something to think about before going to sleep—the next chapter of my internal novel.

Those fantasies seemed innocent at the time and continued into adulthood. However, shortly after I came into a personal relationship with Jesus I began to feel uneasy about them. I couldn't comfortably bring my relationship with Jesus into that kind of fantasy. As I prayed about those self-centered stories, the Lord showed me the ugliness of pride, which the fantasies fostered and the dissatisfaction with real life which they promoted.

I confessed that wishful, prideful activity as sin, as part of the old self that needed to be put aside. I was grateful that God immediately gave me something to put on: the garment of thanksgiving, praise, and prayer to replace the habit of my self-centered creations. Although I was tempted to lapse into the old thought patterns, I chose to use the time to talk with God. Later on I added reviewing Scripture that I had memorized. I had plenty of truth to fill my mind instead of the lies of deceitful dreams.

What needs to be put off and put on can be as unique in detail as any person who needs to change clothing. God has given descriptions in His Word as guidelines to help each one of us discover what aspects of the old self we are still wearing. Some aspects, such as unforgiveness and bitterness, can greatly hinder the walk of a Christian woman and prevent her from walking as gracefully as she could. She can get tangled in the folds of too bulky a costume.

While dancing a solo in front of a large audience, I became acutely aware of the hidden dangers of wearing the wrong clothes. The costume I was wearing had a very full peasant skirt that flowed straight out when I spun around. It was dramatic and elegant with its two tiers of ruffles. The costume worked fantastically well for most of the dance. Then I began a series of difficult turns, *fouette en toumant en dehors*. These turns required me to whip one leg in a wide quarter-circle and to quickly snap it in for each turn while spinning around. Suddenly the skirt started to tangle around my extended leg. The skirt won and I landed on the floor. Fortunately I was able to get up quickly and finish the performance, but I will never forget wearing the wrong apparel.

One passage of Scripture which can be used to test the quality of the clothing that we are wearing is from another letter written by Paul. After encouraging the Ephesian believers to lay aside the old self and put on the new, he gave a description of the actions and attitudes which should follow.

> Therefore, laying aside falsehood, speak truth, each one of you, with his neighbor, for we are members of one another. ... Let no unwholesome word proceed from your mouth, but only such a word as is good for edification according to the need of the moment, that it may give grace to those who hear. And do not grieve the Holy Spirit of God, by whom you were sealed for the day of redemption. Let all bitterness and wrath and anger and clamor and slander be put away from you, along with all malice. And be kind to one another, tenderhearted, forgiving each other, just

as God in Christ also has forgiven you (Ephesians 4:25, 29-32).

I find that my mouth is a pretty reliable indicator of what I happen to be wearing at the moment. If I speak things which are unhelpful or unkind, I know that I have to change clothes. For the Christian, changing clothes on the spot can be quite simple. Going to a private "dressing room" for prayer is useful, though not necessary. Right on the spot I can pray silently to God and confess my sin (wrong attitude, wrong action). Then, because Jesus has provided the way of forgiveness and cleansing, I can put on Christ (His kinds of attitudes and actions). God has made it possible for all of us to be "quick-change artists":

If we confess our sins, He is faithful and righteous to for- give us our sins and to cleanse us from all unrighteousness (1 John 1:9).

I've rushed through lots of costume changes back-stage and nearly missed entrances. Some costumes require a great deal of time to put on and take off. I'm so glad that God, through His Word and through His Holy Spirit, enables me to change spiritual clothes on the spot.

Leotards, tights, and ballet slippers are the dancer's work clothes. Before entering any class or rehearsal, dancers will change garments from street clothes to dancewear. Leotards and tights are like a second skin, providing warmth and freedom of movement. They fit snugly so that both teacher and dancer can see if every part of the body is being used properly for each movement. Ballet costumes are also designed for practical utility. They must allow freedom of movement.

The dancer's shoes are also of utmost importance. In fact, the finest ballet slippers are hand-crafted. For most class work dancers wear the soft ballet slippers, which are made of very flexible leather and fit the foot like a glove. Female dancers also wear satin toe shoes, which are lined with a fabric that has been treated with sizing to make them firm around the toes. The blocked shoes enable the dancer to dance on point—that is, on the very tips of her toes. Occasionally dancers will wear different types of shoes for different characters, but they must fit snugly, weigh very little, and be flexible.

Spiritual clothing is not only graceful and brings forth the beauty of Christ into all kinds of situations, but it is also practical and durable. It is tremendously strong and protective. It is so protective of every part of the believer that Paul called it the full armor of God:

> Put on the full armor of God, that you may be able to stand firm against the schemes of the devil. For the struggle is not against flesh and blood, but against the rulers, against the powers, against the world forces of this darkness, against the spiritual forces of wickedness in the heavenly places. Therefore take up the full armor of God, that you may be able to resist in the evil day, and having done everything, to stand firm. Stand firm therefore, having girded your loins with truth, and having put on the breastplate of righteousness, and having shod your feet with the preparation of the gospel of peace; in addition to all, taking up the shield of faith with which you will be able to extinguish all the flaming missiles of the evil one. And take the helmet of salvation,

and the sword of the Spirit, which is the word of God (Ephesians 6:11-17).

Does doubt take hold of your mind? Put on the helmet of salvation. Does guilt overwhelm you or make you feel inadequate or intimidated? Confess the sin and put on the breastplate of Jesus' righteousness. Are you concerned about being deceived? Put on truth which is found in the Word of God. Are you in difficult circumstances? Put on the shoes of the gospel of peace. Are you being tempted to harbor sinful thoughts, to maintain wrong attitudes, to sin in word or deed? Put on your shield and hold it up. And don't forget to wear your sword, the Word of God. Practice using it, so that it doesn't just hang at your side.

Don't worry about being clothes-conscious. Even Peter encouraged women to adorn themselves with the right kind of clothing:

> Let not your adornment be merely external— braiding the hair, and wearing gold jewelry, or putting on dresses; but let it be the hidden person of the heart, with the imperishable quality of a gentle and quiet spirit, which is precious in the sight of God. For in this way in former times the holy women also, who hoped in God, used to adorn themselves, being submissive to their own husbands (1 Peter 3:3-5).

What flowing garments of love Peter describes here: "a quiet and gentle spirit, which is precious in the sight of God." Let us put off the clothing of the world and put on Christ. Let us please our heavenly Father by wearing His gifts: a quiet and gentle spirit, the armor of God, and the raiments of righteousness and truth.

Devotional Exercise

1. Prayerfully read Psalm 139. Ask God to show you what needs to be put off and what needs to be put on.

2. Confess and receive according to 1 John 1:9.

3. If you have not discovered what God is asking you to put on, review the Bible verses in this chapter and continue to seek God's will for you as you read and think about His Word.

5

Devotion: Motivation of Love

What inspires a ballet dancer to drive herself almost beyond the point of endurance? Why does she continually take classes—at least once a day and sometimes more often—as well as practice on her own and attend rehearsals? What kind of invincible attitude impels her toward excellence even when she is facing difficulties and disappointments?

One driving force behind every dancer who excels is her great passion for dancing—her tremendous devotion to this form of artistic expression. Dancers are not alone in their devotion. Outstanding actors, musicians, artists, and writers are also devoted to their art, not as a thing separate from them, but as an inner part of their being.

Love and devotion are even more central to Christianity than to ballet. The Christian woman may live in a love relationship with God that surpasses any other kind of love. God initiated the relationship: He loved first. He planned before the foundation of the world to provide a way to save what was lost in the Garden and to bring forth sons and daughters through faith in Jesus Christ. The apostle John wrote:

> As many as received Him, to them He gave the right to become children of God, even to those who believe in His name, who were born not of blood, nor of the will of the flesh, nor of the will of man, but of God (John 1:12, 13).

Love for God in response to His love for us is the motivating force behind the Christian woman who excels in walking gracefully with her Lord.

I can remember loving Jesus for as long as I can remember. "Jesus" was a household word, and He was an unseen friend. However, He became much more real to me during the summers that our family spent at Camp Foster. My father worked for the YMCA throughout his adult life, and during my upper-elementary- school years he was a camp director. Camp Foster was right on the shore of Lake Okoboji, near Spirit Lake, Iowa. The woods came right down to the lake and the cabins nestled among the trees. I spent four wonderful summers roaming through the woods and ravines, swimming and canoeing on the lake, playing with other campers, and attending the chapel devotions and campfires.

My dad led the chapel times and also the devotions around the evening campfires. We would sit in a circle around the campfire and sing lively songs. Then we would listen spellbound to the stories of Indians and set- tlers who had lived and died in that very place. Then, as the fire became brighter and the woods became darker, a quiet hush would come over all of us. My dad would begin talking about Jesus, and we would become quiet and thoughtful. Only the soft, irregular crackle of the bonfire and an occasional fish breaking the glassy surface of the water interrupted the profound stillness. I found Jesus with a child's heart there, and I knew that He was with me as I found my way back to the cabin along the thin line of light from a tiny flashlight. His love sustained me throughout my childhood.

When I reached 18, I left childhood things behind. Jesus was a wonderful memory from those happy days, but my collegiate ideas about life did not include Him. I lacked a consistent, Bible-based conception of Jesus. Nevertheless, when Martin and I were married, I was determined for us to attend church. Somehow I still knew that God existed, even though my perception of Him had become distorted.

It was not until after we had our first child, Greg, that I began to know God again. Martin, who had not grown up with any church background, had been attending church out of love and devotion to me rather than for God. But God took us where we were and led us to Himself. One night after Greg had gone to sleep, Martin went into his room and sat looking at our sleeping baby. As he gazed upon Greg and felt tremendous love for him, God revealed His own personal love to Martin and let him know that He loved him as a son too.

Martin was overwhelmed by God's love and determined that we had to find out for ourselves whether or not the Bible was true. This may sound very odd, but we had been attending churches that did not really teach the Bible very much. Although good works were preached with selected Bible passages, I had not grasped the profound meaning of the cross of Christ or salvation by grace. About this same time I was becoming frustrated, because no matter how hard I tried, I was not able to be the good person I thought God wanted me to be. If only I could be good enough, I thought, then perhaps I could have that same kind of love relationship that I had had with Jesus when I was a child.

Martin and I began to read the Bible in earnest. The more we read, the more we were convinced that it was different from other books. It was indeed the inspired Word of God! Finally God led us to a church where the Bible was carefully taught as God's Holy Word, and I became acutely aware that I needed to be saved. I thought I had known Jesus when I was a child, but I had never understood the great truth that Jesus had died to pay the penalty for my sin and to give me new life. Jesus was indeed more than I had ever imagined Him to be! My childhood Jesus was loving, but I had not realized the extent of His love. I am still plumbing the depths of that love which surpasses human comprehension.

I often marvel at the way God arranges things. Just as I had come to know Him in my very childish way at a camp in the woods, I came to know Him as my Lord and Savior at a retreat in another woods. I do not fully understand these two knowings of Him, but I am convinced that He has His hand on each one who will be His. He gives us the light we are able to receive at each point along the way.

This may be a roundabout way of talking about devotion to God, but devotion is personal. Each of us has a story to tell about how God started the devotion: how

He called us, how He revealed Himself to us, how He saved us, and how He brought us into a love relationship with Himself. Devotion to God comes out of a profound relationship with the One who gave His life as a ransom for many. The devotion started with God's love, not mine and not yours. He is the One who loved first. Then, as we respond to His love, we love Him back.

> In this is love, not that we loved God, but that He loved us and sent His Son to be the propitiation for our sins (1 John 4:10).

Loving God involves obedience to His Word. If we love Him, we love His Word and obey His commands. Jesus said:

> He who has My commandments and keeps them, he it is who loves Me. ... If anyone loves Me, he will keep My word. ... He who does not love Me does not keep My words (John 14:21, 23, 24).

Obeying Jesus' commandments does not bring about our salvation, for we cannot earn it. Nor do we obey in order to earn His love or to obtain His favor. We obey Him because we love Him. We obey Him because we trust that His words come from His perfect love and we desire to respond to His love in devotion.

The more devoted a dancer is to ballet, the more she strives to improve her skill and artistic expression. And the more she excels, the more devoted to ballet she becomes. Likewise, the Christian woman who loves Jesus and thereby obeys Him will grow in her graciousness—her expression of God's truth and beauty. The more she reflects on His love for her, the more she loves Him back.

The more she grows into the image of Jesus, the more she relies on His love for her. The more she looks at His loving ways, the more she becomes like Him. There is a glorious snowball effect: The more she looks at Him and receives His love, the more she loves Him and wants to obey Him. The closer she gets, the more she loves Him, until He becomes all in all and her life is truly the image of His grace and beauty.

The dancer who is devoted to ballet dances even when she does not feel like it. The Christian woman who is devoted to God obeys His commandments even when she does not feel like it. If obedience becomes drudgery, she needs to look again at Christ's love for her. She needs to remember His love while He hung on the cross. She needs to remember that He intercedes for her before the Father. She needs to look at Him more than at her circumstances. Then she will renew her love for Him.

Sometimes we are encouraged and even persuaded to focus on our feelings, but feelings come and go; the focus must return to Jesus. In Him we find the love that truly sustains us. True love, in devotion and commitment, remains and sustains us as we choose to walk in God's grace. God never asks us to deny the existence of feelings, but He calls us to a passion of love and devotion that will surpass and overcome those feelings which would interfere with the dance of love.

Anything less than devotion to God will fail when things get rough. We had a secondhand glimpse of the extent of hardship that can be endured in the strength of God's love and the believer's devotion. Martin, the children, and I had the privilege of driving a retired missionary by the name of Mary Lewer back and forth for church three times a week for several years. She shared herself and told her story in bits and pieces along the way. Even after the difficult hardships and the great tragedies she had endured, there was such a commitment of down-to-earth devotion about her that she seemed invincible. She was bearing fruit in her old age, and that fruit was the tremendous influence she had on all our lives.

Only a burning passion for Jesus could have sustained Mary Lewer through the years of hardship among the Lisu people of the mountain region of inland China. She and her husband, Alfred, had both been called by God to preach to people who had never heard the gospel of Jesus. After enduring the hardships of learning the language and becoming accustomed to the vast differences in living conditions, they settled first in Tibet and then moved across the border to Weihsi, in the mountainous region of inland China. They lost their baby boy soon after he was born, and yet they stayed on. Mary's sister Ada joined them at the mission station, and the work grew rapidly. Then after some fruitful years of ministry and many souls won to Christ, they felt the need for more workers in the area. Mary Lewer took the long journey—three weeks by mule, then many days by train, then weeks by boat—to England to inspire workers to come to China.

After Mary returned to the mission, she and Alfred made plans to meet the Boltons, the young couple that had responded to the challenge to join the work among the Lisu people. Preparations were made for Alfred Lewer and his closest Lisu worker, Pastor David Ho, to begin the long journey to meet the Boltons. But Alfred Lewer never completed the journey. While Mary eagerly awaited the arrival of the new missionaries and while the Boltons waited for Alfred to meet them in Burma, Pastor Ho saw his beloved missionary friend swept away in the Mekong River.

Pastor Ho continued the journey alone to meet the Boltons. He did meet them, and after many weeks they reached the mission station to join the new widow, her children, and her sister Ada. By this time Mary had two little daughters, Katherine and Eleanor. How could she continue on in China without her husband? Wouldn't it be logical for her to return to her own homeland in the hills of Pennsylvania? Logical, yes, but her love for Jesus and for the Lisu people whom He had put in her care kept her in China. She had come to serve her Lord, and she would stay.

Mary Lewer stayed in China with only a few furloughs, one of which was enforced by political problems. She continued while her daughters grew into womanhood. She eagerly looked forward to the day when Katherine would complete her Bible school training and join her in China. Katherine did return to serve Jesus alongside her mother, but after only a short while she became ill and died. Yet Mary knew what it had cost the Father to give His only-begotten Son to save many souls, and so she stayed on as long as she could.

We saw in Mary Lewer a down-to-earth, practical devotion to Jesus. She was not at all ethereal, but stalwart in her commitment to her Lord. She knew how to laugh at herself and was not afraid to admit her mistakes and failings. Whenever she spoke, she expressed the faithfulness of God. And in doing so, she often related her own temporary failings along the path of trusting God in every detail. She told of one incident that had happened when they were traveling in a caravan. They had been delayed in a small village an extra day, and she confessed, "I fussed in my spirit and I fussed in my spirit." Little did she realize at the time that the Lord had been sparing them, for if they had traveled with the caravan the day they had planned, they would have been robbed by the bandits. She would shake her head and say again, "And there I was fussing in my spirit while all along God was taking care of us."

Mary Lewer always wanted to be sure that she elevated the love and faithfulness of God rather than her own goodness. She did this because she knew Him intimately and had received much of His love and grace. She did this because her whole life was a love relationship with Jesus. She loved Him more than anyone or anything else. She loved Him more than life itself.

When God calls a person to a difficult task, He knows that faithfulness and commitment to do His will can only be possible through love. That is why Jesus asked Peter, "Do you love Me more than these?" Jesus knew that even love for people would be inadequate to sustain and enable Peter to face the greatest odds. Peter had to love Jesus more than anyone or anything else—even more than the sheep and lambs which God would entrust to him.

Devotion to God also sustains us through difficult circumstances. Peter wrote a letter to Christians who were suffering persecution and who were being sustained by their devotion to God as well as by the indwelling Holy Spirit. After reviewing the truths of their salvation and their living hope of resurrection and eternal life with Jesus, he wrote:

> In this you greatly rejoice, even though now for a little while, if necessary, you have been distressed by various trials, that the proof of your faith, being more precious than gold which is perishable, even though tested by fire, may be found to result in praise and glory and honor at the revelation of Jesus Christ; and though you have not seen Him, you love Him, and though you do not see Him now, but believe in Him, you greatly rejoice with joy inexpressible and full of glory, obtaining as the outcome of your faith the salvation of your souls (1 Peter 1:6-9).

Only single-minded devotion for God can result in the kind of faithfulness which brings joy in the midst of trial.

Love is expressed through faithful obedience. Devotion may also be developed through engaging in thoughts, words, and actions which are consistent with God's will as expressed in His Word. Doing the will of God both expresses love and develops devotion, so that when the difficulties come, the devotion and commitment enable us to remain faithful. Love is far more than emotion: It includes the mind, will, and action as well. Love continues when feelings fail. Love is doing the will of God no matter what the consequences are.

Mary of Bethany loved Jesus beyond life itself. When she anointed Him with the very costly ointment of spikenard, it was as though she was pouring out her very life for Him. Jesus knew her heart and received her devotion.

I have often wondered just how much she understood
about what Jesus had to face that final week.

Did she know
as with broken heart
she cracked open the box,
treasure saved
for her own death?

Did she know
as she mingled fragrance
with tears
penetrating His heart,
spikenard prepared Him
for death?

Did she know
as she wiped ointment
with cascades of hair,
lingering aroma
would tell of her love
through betrayal,
trial, scourging?

Did she know
as the cruelty of unjust
death stretched His love,
nothing could annihilate
her gift?

Did she know
as He was pierced,
His gift poured out to her
fragrance of hope,
essence of eternity?

Only the Christian who loves her Lord more than anyone or anything else will find fullness of joy and contentment in the midst of trial. Only the Christian who loves Jesus with all her heart, soul, mind, and strength will do great exploits for God.

Devotional Exercise

1. Prayerfully read Psalm 145. Write down the action words which express the writer's love for God.

2. List all the ways that you can think of to bless the Lord through words and actions.

3. We develop devotion for God through our thoughts, words, and actions. What thoughts, words, and actions might you engage in to increase your devotion for God?

6

Attitudes for Excellence

Three other characteristics accompany devotion: a teachable attitude, determination, and perseverance. For a dancer to excel, she must be teachable. This sounds obvious, but those who resist correction will not improve beyond a certain point. The dancer who is truly devoted to ballet is eager for correction because she wants to perform each step as well as possible. Humility is a great part of that teachable attitude, while pride interferes with learning.

Determination enables a dancer to overcome such obstacles as boredom over repetition. Determination is goal-related. However, the goal does not have to be a far-reaching one. Sometimes just the desire to do a better quadruple pirouette with a secure landing will drive a dancer to spend hours and hours for days and weeks practicing pirouettes. In ballet a person never runs out of possible goals for improvement. If a dancer can leap (grand jeté) a good distance at a high elevation with every part of her body in perfect position and land with grace and sure placement, she can always strive for greater distance and higher elevation. Even the greatest dancers have unreached goals stimulating them with determination to conquer the yet-unconquered.

Perseverance is that day-by-day, repetitious willingness to keep on keeping on. Without perseverance, determination would lag, because it is the perseverance—over-and-over repetition—that leads toward the goal. It's like climbing a mountain: The desire to reach the top and the challenge to reach the summit stimulate determination, but it's the perseverance that takes each step. Perseverance takes over when enthusiasm fades and when frustration and discouragement come along. The goal of perfecting a certain step often seems closer than it actually is. To reach that goal, the dancer must be teachable, determined, and persevering.

By now you have probably guessed some of the spiritual implications. A teachable spirit, determination to follow Christ all the way, and perseverance under trial are all essential aspects of walking in God's grace. It is by His grace that we are able to walk successfully, for He gives us ample opportunities to develop these attitudes of the heart.

Teachability

The woman of God will keep herself tender toward the Lord and teachable, ready, and eager to learn His will and active to obey. In his book *With Christ in the School of Obedience*, Andrew Murray wrote:

The true pupil, say of some great musician or painter, yields his master a whole-hearted and unhesitating submission.

In practicing his scales or mixing his colors, in the slow and patient study of the elements of his art, he knows that it is wisdom simply and fully to obey.

It is this wholehearted surrender to His guidance, this implicit submission to His authority which Christ asks. We come to Him asking Him to teach us the lost art of obeying God as He did.

Obedience to the Lord is essential in the process of learning. One of the most beautiful pictures of a teachable woman is found in the Gospel of Luke:

Now as they were traveling along, He entered a certain village; and a woman named Martha welcomed Him into her home. And she had a sister called Mary, who moreover was listening to the Lord's word, seated at His feet (Luke 10:38, 39).

Mary's attitude of devotion made her teachable. She had a hunger to know Jesus, a thirst to know God. Her focus of attention was not on herself, but on Jesus. Her humility as a learner (a disciple) could be seen even in her posture and place—seated at the feet of Jesus.

Mary was also a listener. Every word penetrated her heart and she received her Lord's words with faith. She was absorbed in what the Teacher was saying rather than in herself. She was so intent on Jesus' words that she didn't even notice her poor sister, who was beside herself with preparations and irritations. Mary didn't hear the pans clanging or notice the pointed looks that Martha shot across the room.

In contrast to Mary's receptivity to all that Jesus said, Martha bustled around barely hearing a word from the Lord:

> But Martha was distracted with all her preparations; and she came up to Him, and said, "Lord, do You not care that my sister has left me to do all the serving alone? Then tell her to help me" (Luke 10:40).

Martha was filled with her own ideas about how to serve Jesus. Moreover, she had inadvertently placed her own activities and plans before the Word of God.

Too much to do in too little time can tempt a woman to ignore or postpone learning at the feet of Jesus. Necessary chores and good works can even stand in the way of listening to God. And when she does not listen to Him or learn His ways, she can become resentful and frustrated about all the work she has to do. She can become as distracted as Martha and then complain to the Lord and accuse Him of not caring. The audacity of Martha's accusation and demand burst from a heart too full to listen.

Jesus, however, did not want Martha to miss out on learning, so He gave her a special opportunity to become a learner.

> The Lord answered and said to her, "Martha, Martha, you are worried and bothered about so

many things; but only a few things are necessary really only one, for Mary has chosen the good part, which shall not be taken away from her" (Luke 10:41).

Martha thought she was doing what was necessary and important. Jesus gently but directly let her know that what she was doing paled in comparison to listening and learning the Word of God. Luke does not describe Martha's reaction. Did she internally say "Humph!" and turn on her heel? Or did she just stand there in abject embarrassment? Did she glare at Mary? Did she excuse or justify herself?

I believe that Martha was initially stunned, but that she softened to receive the rebuke which was given in love. Mary had indeed taken the better part—that of a student of the Word. When Martha realized the impact of Jesus' rebuke, she did not recoil but took up the challenge. She too would learn from the Master. She loved Him and held Him in high esteem. Otherwise she would not have invited Jesus and His disciples to her house and become overwhelmed with preparing food and serving.

Mary chose to sit at Jesus' feet to learn as much as she could. Martha was jolted into learning. And that is indeed how we learn: Sometimes we choose to learn and at other times we are externally motivated. Mary had chosen the good part of learning, and Jesus said that what she learned would not be taken away. Martha learned the hard way and yet she would also remember. Both became learners and doers of the Word.

It is far easier for a dancer to recognize error and even receive criticism from her teacher than it is for a person to recognize a personal fault and to respond favorably to criticism. Yet in the Christian walk the Lord is in the process of changing each one of us. Since He includes us in the change process, we do have to face personal shortcomings. When we do, He shows us what to change and gives us the ability to do it.

The Lord teaches through His Word. Then He gives us opportunities to practice what we are learning. As we are learning we also discover changes that need to be made. Each time we recognize the shortcoming or sin and confess it to Him, He helps us make the correction and gives us further opportunities to practice what we are learning.

> All Scripture is inspired by God and profitable for teaching, for reproof, for correction, for training in righteousness; that the man of God may be adequate, equipped for every good work (2 Timothy 3:16,17).

Reading the Word of God and learning the principles of Scripture from an intellectual point of view are not enough. Reading must be accompanied by humility and faith and then learned through obedience to the Word.

A teachable attitude is such that it receives reproof and correction as well as instruction. Mary revealed the teachable attitude of a receptive, listening heart during instruction. Martha, on the other hand, showed that she also had a teachable attitude, for she took Jesus' rebuke and correction and came under His training in righteousness. It is far too easy to remember Martha as the woman overwhelmed with trivialities and duties. A "Martha" title is assigned to women who slave in the kitchen, but never to one who has a teachable spirit. How sad! Martha did not remain in her busy distraction of too much to do without enough help. Martha took the Lord's instruction and became a listener and learner along with her sister. Both women became equipped for every good work, even for work in the kitchen.

Martha indeed became an avid student of the Lord. How do we know this? The apostle John records her words of faith after the death of her brother Lazarus. When Lazarus became ill, Martha and Mary sent for Jesus. However, the traveling time was such that, by the time Jesus received the summons, He knew that He would not reach Bethany until two days after Lazarus' death. Therefore Jesus delayed an additional two days so that Martha, Mary, and His disciples could see the glory of God.

As soon as Martha heard that Jesus was approaching, she gathered herself up out of grief and hurried to Him. Her words of faith were as strong and rich as those of any disciple or apostle: "Lord, if You had been here, my brother would not have died." This is not a rebuke or even a complaint. It is a statement of profound faith in the Son of God. Jesus' conversation with Martha then brought forth more words of faith.

> Jesus said to her, "Your brother shall rise again."

> Martha said to Him, "I know that he will rise again in the resurrection on the last day"

> Jesus said to her, "I am the resurrection and the life; he who believes in Me shall live even if he

> dies, and everyone who lives and believes in Me
> shall never die. Do you believe this?"

> She said to Him, "Yes, Lord; I have believed that
> You are the Christ, the Son of God, even He who
> comes into the world" (John 11:23-27).

Martha identified Jesus as the Christ, the Son of God. She
had become so teachable that she had received divine
truth—truth that no person, no doubt, no circumstance
could snatch away.

Martha then went to Mary and said, "The Teacher is
here, and is calling for you." As soon as Mary heard this
she rose quickly, followed Martha, and fell at Jesus' feet.
Mary had also continued to be teachable. Her first words
were identical to Martha's: "Lord, if You had been here,
my brother would not have died." Jesus did not examine
Mary's faith in the same way He had Martha s. Mary's
faith was deep and abiding. She said it all with her eyes
and her manner.

Both women had thus far received instruction.
Martha had needed reproof and correction. Both had
continued their training in righteousness. Jesus knew
they were ready for further training—to obey His voice
when everything militated against it.

> Jesus therefore, again being deeply moved
> within, came to the tomb. Now it was a cave, and
> a stone was lying against it.

> Jesus said, "Remove the stone."

Martha, the sister of the deceased, said to Him, "Lord, by this time there will be a stench, for he has been dead four days."

Jesus said to her, "Did I not say to you, if you believe, you will see the glory of God?" And so they removed the stone (John 11:38-41).

At first Martha objected, but then by sheer faith in Jesus, she obeyed His words and consented to have the stone removed. The disciples also believed and removed the stone.

Training in righteousness brings forth miracles in peoples lives as faith becomes strong and obedience becomes the life- style.

And so they removed the stone. And Jesus raised His eyes and said, "Father, I thank Thee that Thou heardest Me. And I knew that Thou hearest Me always; but because of the people standing around I said it, that they may believe that Thou didst send Me." And when He had said these things, He cried out with a loud voice, "Lazarus, come forth."

He who had died came forth, bound hand and foot with wrappings; and his face was wrapped around with a cloth. Jesus said to them, "Unbind him, and let him go."

Many therefore of the Jews, who had come to Mary and beheld what He had done, believed in Him. But some of them went away to the

Pharisees, and told them the things which Jesus had done (John 11:41-46).

This certainly is an illustration of what Jesus meant when He said, "Whoever has, to him shall more be given" (Mark 4:25). The more Mary and Martha learned in faith the more they were able to receive and believe.

A teachable attitude should continue into old age. A mature Christian is never too old to learn. One day our missionary friend Mary Lewer, who was then in her nineties, revealed her teachable attitude. Her rent had been raised and she was very concerned about it, since her pension was small. She had begun to complain to the Lord about this, and He had gently rebuked her: "Trust me in this. Thank me for what you have." As an act of willful obedience she began to thank God for the way the landlord kept the grass trimmed. She thanked God for the bright flowers that bordered the green grass. She obeyed God's Word: "In everything give thanks; for this is God's will for you in Christ Jesus" (1 Thessalonians 5:18). As she thanked Him with her will, her faith settled in and she was renewed in peace. The learning had once again taken hold.

Mary Lewer did not place her faith in a prayer that the rent would be reduced. She placed her faith in her Provider. A few days later she was delightfully surprised with news that the landlord had changed his mind. Mary Lewer, a woman who had lived by faith throughout her entire life of dedicated service, continued her training in righteousness and saw the evidence of His faithfulness—first by faith, then by sight.

Determination

Mary and Martha of Bethany and Mary Lewer were not only teachable, but they acted with determination. Paul revealed his heart attitude of determination in his letter to the Philippians. He too had been jolted into becoming a disciple. In complete humility he had set aside his pomp and circumstance—a Pharisee of Pharisees—and become a learner who was determined above all else to know Jesus intimately through obedience and service.

> Whatever things were gain to me, those things I have counted as loss for the sake of Christ. More than that, I count all things to be loss in view of the surpassing value of knowing Christ Jesus my Lord, for whom I have suffered the loss of all things, and count them but rubbish in order that I may gain Christ, and may be found in Him, not having a righteousness of my own derived from the Law, but that which is through faith in Christ, the righteousness which comes from God on the basis of faith, that I may know Him, and the power of His resurrection and the fellowship of His sufferings, being conformed to His death; in order that I may attain to the resurrection from the dead (Philippians 3:7-11).

Paul's determination to know Christ was not merely an intellectual quest. Paul was motivated by single-minded devotion to know Him as fully as He might be known. Paul understood that to know Him is to obey Him. Obedience is intrinsic to knowing Him. Yet the obedience to do all that Jesus said came not from Paul's own righteousness, which he counted as worthless.

Paul's obedience was the response of relationship and was therefore comprised of righteousness from God through faith.

Paul's determination was not a grit-your-teeth-and-bear-it kind of doggedness. The goal of knowing Christ in greater fullness motivated him in such a way as to overshadow all other distractions and lesser desires. That is why he said he counted what might be considered something in this world as nothing in comparison to "the surpassing value of knowing Christ Jesus."

Do you want to know Jesus as much as Paul did? Do you want to know and please Him more than anything else in life? Jesus said that we cannot serve two masters, and James wrote that a double-minded man is unstable in all his ways. Paul had one all-consuming goal: to know Jesus. He was fully determined to devote himself to knowing Him.

I must confess that lesser goals have often taken precedence in my life and that I have put other desires and other people before Christ. When I discover that I have set aside my primary goal for lesser concerns, I must confess my sin and re-prioritize my life so that all that I am and do is refocused on the goal of knowing and glorifying God.

Several years ago I decided to devote a full hour to prayer every day—60 consecutive minutes. The first few days were wonderful—devoid of distractions since the children were all in school. Then came Saturday. With at least a tinge of other-worldliness I announced my intention to go back to the bedroom for an hour of prayer. With great determination I marched back to our bedroom, closed the door behind me, and began to pray—with the wrong attitude. My focus had slipped off of Jesus and onto myself and what I was doing. After a few minor interruptions at the door I was completely frustrated and angry. My determination to pray rather than to know Jesus through prayer slipped into self-righteous disobedience. When I finally realized that I was sinning instead of obeying, my prayer became real: Forgive me, Lord, cleanse me and renew a right spirit within me.

Someone has said that it is better to obey than to pray, but I believe that both are imperative and must work together. When I prayed for my Lord to show me the way to obey He answered. I was then able to spend time with Him without becoming angry or upset with the circumstances. That day gave me practice in praying always, even in the midst of interruptions and turmoil. The desire to know Him had to take precedence over my own ideas concerning prayer and obedience. The epistle to the Hebrews reminds us:

> We do not have a high priest who cannot sympathize with our weaknesses, but one who has been tempted in all things as we are, yet without sin. Let us therefore draw near with confidence to the throne of grace, that we may receive mercy and may find grace to help in time of need (Hebrews 4:15, 16).

Indeed we need to spend quiet time with the Lord, but we also need to know how to pray in the midst of life's interruptions "to find grace to help in time of need." We need to determine to know Jesus in every thought, every attitude, and every circumstance so that He might be preeminent in all things.

Perseverance

Perseverance works hand in hand with determination. If we compare determination with keeping the eye on the goal, we could say that perseverance is made up of each step taken along the way Paul kept his eyes on the goal and persevered. Even after he had proceeded further along the way than most of us, he confessed:

> Not that I have already obtained it, or have already become perfect, but I press on in order that I may lay hold of that for which also I was laid hold of by Christ Jesus. Brethren, I do not regard myself as having laid hold of it yet; but one thing I do: forgetting what lies behind and reaching forward to what lies ahead, I press on toward the goal for the prize of the upward call of God in Christ Jesus (Philippians 3:12-14).

And indeed Paul pressed on! He never flinched in spite of floggings. We have the record of his first missionary journey. After his preaching in the synagogue at Antioch of Pisidia, contention arose. The Jews who did not agree with his message incited the mob to drive Paul and his companions out of town. Paul and the others proceeded to Iconium. Again many believed, but others organized a plot against Paul and nearly stoned him to death. Paul and his companions went on to Lycaonia, Lystra, and Derbe, where many eagerly received the good news. But enemies from Pisidian Antioch and Iconium came and enflamed the people against Paul: "They stoned Paul and dragged him out of the city, supposing him to be dead" (Acts 14:19). However, when the believers stood around Paul he rose up and returned to the city.

Paul could have chosen a different route back to Tarsus and the Antioch church (not to be confused with Antioch of Pisidia). Paul and his companions could easily have traveled by way of the Cilician Gates, a natural pass through the mountains, located southeast of Derbe. Paul, however, persevered with the work that God had assigned to him. He returned the long, hard way— back through Derbe, Iconium, and Antioch of Pisidia to strengthen the new believers and to establish them in the faith. Paul continued to persevere. Further evidence of his persistence can be seen in his second letter to the Corinthians.

> Are they servants of Christ? (I speak as if insane) I more so; in far more labors, in far more imprisonments, beaten times without number, often in danger of death. Five times I received from the Jews thirty-nine lashes. Three times I was beaten with rods, once I was stoned, three times I was shipwrecked, a night and a day I have spent in the deep. I have been on frequent journeys, in dangers from rivers, dangers from robbers, dangers from my countrymen, dangers from the Gentiles, dangers in the city, dangers in the wilderness, dangers on the sea, dangers among false brethren; I have been in labor and hardship, through many sleepless nights, in hunger and thirst, often without food, in cold and exposure. Apart from such external things, there

is the daily pressure upon me of concern for all the churches (2 Corinthians 11:23-28).

Missionaries must count the cost and have the same perseverance, because they meet similar trials. Most of us have not had to continue in faith through such severe circumstances. Nevertheless, we must also be ready to persevere. Our life is not our own anymore; we belong to Jesus.

> The love of Christ controls us, having concluded this, that one died for all, therefore all died; and He died for all, that they who live should no longer live for themselves, but for Him who died and rose again on their behalf (2 Corinthians 5:14, 15).

> Not one of us lives for himself, and not one dies for himself; for if we live, we live for the Lord, or if we die, we die for the Lord; therefore whether we live or die, we are the Lord's (Romans 14:7, 8).

Indeed Paul took Jesus' words seriously:

> If anyone wishes to come after Me, let him deny himself, and take up his cross, and follow Me. For whoever wishes to save his life shall lose it; but whoever loses his life for My sake shall find it (Matthew 16:24, 25).

The woman of God has a higher calling than that of a ballerina. The woman who belongs to Jesus has a more compelling reason to be teachable. She has a far greater purpose to be determined to follow Jesus all the way and to persevere no matter what the cost. The ballerina gives her life to her art, which will fade as the grass. The woman of God gives her life to the Lord for His glory and His purpose unto eternal life.

When the ballerina has passed her physical and artistic peak, she will only have memories. When the Christian woman passes through youth and enters old age she continues to press on to the mark of the "high calling of God in Christ Jesus." She has a hope that extends beyond this life—a hope that brings love and joy even out of the most difficult circumstances. She can heartily agree with Paul:

> Having been justified by faith, we have peace with God through our Lord Jesus Christ, through whom also we have obtained our introduction by faith into this grace in which we stand; and we exult in hope of the glory of God. And not only this, but we also exult in our tribulations, knowing that tribulation brings about perseverance; and perseverance, proven character; and proven character, hope; and hope does not disappoint, because the love of God has been poured out within our hearts through the Holy Spirit who was given to us (Romans 5:1-5).

And when she reaches her goal, she will see her Lord face-to- face. She will know Him and she will be like Him:

> Beloved, now we are children of God, and it has not appeared as yet what we shall be. We know that, when He appears, we shall be like Him,

because we shall see Him just as He is (1 John 3:2).

Devotional Exercise

1. Read Proverbs 1:1-9; 2:1-11; and 4:1-27. Describe a person who is truly teachable.

2. Read Philippians 3:7-14. Pray about your goals and write them down. What are you going to do about them beginning right now?

3. Read Romans 5:1-5. How does a person develop perseverance?

7

Five Ballet Positions: Prayer

The floor is bare except for smudges of resin here and there. Reflections from the mirror-lined walls give the illusion of repeated space divided into regular sections by horizontal ballet *barres*. The waiting silence is only slightly disturbed by one dancer. She enters the room and resolutely walks over to the *barre* to prepare for class. She drapes her towel across it and bends over to adjust her shoe.

Other dancers join her. Some gather in groups and talk in hushed voices. A few plop down onto the floor to stretch tight muscles. Others lightly practice a few steps or begin warming up. The scene is random until the teacher taps the floor with a stick. The dancers take their positions at the *barre*. Suddenly strict uniformity replaces the former random variety. The transformation is startling. It is as though scattered bits of wool have suddenly jumped into the shape of a neatly knitted scarf.

The freedom of movement during performance originates from the traditional regimentation of classical ballet. Although there are slight differences between the classical Ceccetti method and other standardized techniques, ballet training follows strict rules in the position and execution of every pose and movement.

Five basic body positions predominate. Each position requires both the inner and upward pull of the body as well as an outward expression. The dancer centers her body, but each position is created for outward expression to an audience. Therefore the legs and arms are turned outward. The outward stance provides stability, agility and the ability to move quickly in different directions. The dancer is thus able to perform much of the dance while facing the audience.

Christians also have a basis for inner stability and outward expression. Rather than moving through life in a random fashion, independently doing their own thing, women of God are called into a life of conformity to the will of God. Although each woman is unique, the steps of grace, the promises of God, and the fruit of the Spirit are the same for all. God calls us into harmony with His will, which comes from the profound relationship of love. Our relationship with the Father gives us stability and direction in order to help us express His love to those around us. The inner and outer position of the Christian is summed up in the Great Commandment to love God with all our being and to love others as well. If every inner attitude and thought are within the bounds of love for God, then the external expression will reflect the internal relationship.

Just as the five basic positions in ballet have both inner strength and outward expression, relationship and communication with God through prayer have both inner strength and external results. Although prayer may be hidden away in the privacy of our hearts, the results become visible. They are seen not only as answers to prayer but also in the fruit of the Spirit. The more we are in communion with the Father and the more we consider Him, the more we reflect His character qualities of love, expressed in grace and truth.

In their most basic form, the five ballet positions have the weight evenly distributed on both feet. In each position the feet and legs are turned out from the hips. In First Position the backs of the heels touch each other. Because the legs are turned outward, the feet very nearly form one single line so that the shoulders are directly over the toes. Second Position retains the same line, but the feet are separated by a space of about one foot. The actual distance between the feet is in proportion to the size of the dancer.

Third Position is assumed by bringing one foot slightly in front of the other so that the heel of one foot snuggles up against the arch of the other foot. Fourth Position is an open position with one foot in front of and parallel to the other. One heel is in front of the toes of the opposite foot. As the dancer draws the feet together from fourth position she will assume Fifth Position, with the legs slightly crossed so that one foot is almost directly in front of the other with the toes of each foot pressed against the heel of the other. Beginners can only approximate the positions because they have not yet developed an adequate turnout in which the knees are in line with the toes. Once the five basic positions of the feet and legs are learned, the arms are also placed in the corresponding positions.

Because of the great importance of the ballet positions and because they illustrate both inner strength and preparation for outward movement, they remind me of prayer. Just as a dancer cannot truly dance without being established in these positions, a Christian cannot truly walk in the Spirit without prayer. Moving in and out of these positions with the habit of turning the legs out eventually becomes automatic for a dancer. Likewise, moving in and out of prayer should become the habitual activity of every daughter of God. Such a habit can be developed only by constant practice.

Even the most advanced dancer continues to work on maintaining the correct stance in each of the positions. Likewise, a mature Christian woman sets her mind to pray at regular times so that prayer will continue to be an automatic response during the day Prayer is like a reference point—turning to God, who is the very source of our being.

Although most of my dance training was in strict classical ballet, I did study modern dance as well. Certain habits which I had developed in ballet tended to intrude. Many of these habits were extremely useful for balance, ease of movement, and rapid comprehension. However, the turnout of the five ballet positions labeled me as a ballet dancer. The instructor teased me about my habit of automatically dancing in the turned out position and utilizing the five positions of ballet.

Wouldn't it be wonderful to have such a habit of prayer? Wouldn't it be wonderful to be criticized for walking too closely with God? That's what prayer is all about: walking closely with God. It is consulting Him on everything. It is unburdening the heart and listening to His voice on the inside. It is regarding Him and giving heed to His will. It is calling on Him in desperate need and turning to Him in the routines of life. It is asking, seeking, and knocking. It is also thanking, praising, and worshiping.

For a dancer to learn to stand in each position properly she must have a model. She must see others standing in those positions. The Bible is full of models of prayer. It is full of both pray-ers and prayers. The Bible is an extended record of prayer. God communed with Adam in the Garden. Enoch walked with God. Noah heard God's specific directions for building the ark. Moses was continually in communication with God during the final 40 years of his life. Hannah wept before God and received a son who served God as priest and prophet. King David was a man of prayer and praise. Isaiah, Jeremiah, Ezekiel, Daniel, and the other prophets were men of prayer. How else could they have heard God? How else could they have known that the voice they heard was God's voice? Elizabeth, Mary and Anna were women of prayer who received the promise of God. But, more than all of these, Jesus prayed.

Ballet students benefit greatly by having more advanced students demonstrate how a position or step should be done. Christians have the perfect model: Jesus Christ Himself! He is our perfect model for prayer. He lived a life of prayer and of constant communication with the Father. And, although He went to secluded places to pray in secret, His lines of communication were always open to the Father.

Jesus prayed to the Father and urged His disciples to pray Jesus did nothing without prayer. He did nothing without complete and active dependence on and unity with the Father. Our only glimpse into His boyhood illustrates His early prayer life. After celebrating the Feast of the Passover, His parents were returning home when they discovered that He was not in the group as they had supposed. When they returned to Jerusalem they found Him in the temple. Jesus' answer to their rebuke was, "Why is it that you were looking for Me? Did you not know that I had to be in My Father's house?" (Luke 2:49). The next recorded incident in Jesus' life was His baptism. Again we see Him in prayer:

> It came about when all the people were baptized, that Jesus also was baptized, and while He was praying, heaven was opened, and the Holy Spirit descended upon Him in bodily form like a dove, and a voice came out of heaven, "Thou art My beloved Son, in Thee I am well-pleased" (Luke 3:21, 22)

Although this was the beginning of His public ministry it was not the beginning of His prayer life. His entire life was lived in communion with the Father.

Prayer can be sweet communion, and it can be affirming because of the tremendous love relationship between God and His child. However, our next encounter with Jesus illustrates another aspect of prayer, that of praying through difficult times of testing:

> Jesus, full of the Holy Spirit, returned from the Jordan and was led about by the Spirit in the wilderness for forty days, being tempted by the devil. And He ate nothing during those days; and when they had ended, He became hungry (Luke 4:1, 2).

How is one "led about by the Spirit" except through prayer? Furthermore, we know He was praying because He was fasting. Before beginning any venture with God by faith, Jesus went aside to pray. This time it was for 40 days and nights. Before we begin any work for God, however large or small, we too must turn aside and seek God in prayer.

Jesus was in obedience and He was in prayer. Yet in the midst of His obedience and prayer the devil dared to approach Him. Prayer does not keep the devil away, but it prepares one for battle. Jesus was prepared because of His habit of prayer. The battle had to be won in prayer before it could be won among men. This is the same for each of us.

As we read through the Gospels we find Jesus praying over and over again: before any decision, before any action; sometimes privately sometimes publicly. Even though most of His praying was in the privacy of His heart and often in a secluded spot, His disciples noticed that Jesus prayed. They asked Him to teach them to pray Jesus did not explain how to pray, nor can anyone truly explain prayer. Instead He said, "Pray then, in this way." He demonstrated prayer.

The Lord's Prayer compresses awesome communion with God into just a few words. With astounding brevity

Jesus expressed love and reverence for God and prayed for the will of God and the needs of humanity

> Our Father who art in heaven,
> Hallowed be Thy name.
> Thy kingdom come.
> Thy will be done
> On earth as it is in heaven.
> Give us this day our daily bread.
> And forgive us our debts, as we also
> have forgiven our debtors.
> And do not lead us into temptation,
> But deliver us from evil
> (Matthew 6:9-13).

The Lord's Prayer begins with relationship and worship. The first two requests are in complete agreement with God's purposes. The final requests sum up the basic needs of the Christian: physical sustenance, forgiveness, and the help we so desperately need to keep from sinning. The final requests also reveal the Lord as mankind's source for help.

The Lord's Prayer serves as a model and form for prayer. It also reminds me of the five positions of ballet, because it includes five basic positions in which to move in prayer. In every position the primary focus is upon God.

First Position

The First Position of prayer is that of relationship to the Father. The awesome nature of the relationship is condensed in two phrases: "Our Father" and "Hallowed be Thy name." It is the relationship of a holy God with a mere mortal who has been rescued out of the kingdom of darkness and transformed into a child of God.

Prayer is *relationship*; it is not mere words. Neither is it simply repetition of requests. Prayer is communion with the Creator and Sustainer of the universe. Prayer is being in the presence of righteousness, holiness, justice, truth, mercy, power, and love. Prayer is both at the foot of the cross of Jesus Christ and before the throne of our Almighty Father. Jesus prayed that we might be one with the Father even as He is one with the Father. We have been called into this profound relationship in which we may simply converse with God.

The first two words, "Our Father," establish the basis and purpose of all prayer, that of relationship. Even asking, seeking, and knocking for God's intervention in our lives depends upon our relationship with Him. Oswald Chambers, in his well-known daily devotional book, *My Utmost for His Highest*, goes so far as to say "The idea of prayer is not in order to get answers from God; prayer is perfect and complete oneness with God." He advises:

> Think of the last thing you prayed about—were you devoted to your desire or to God? Determined to get some gift of the Spirit or to get at God? "Your Heavenly Father knoweth what things ye have need of before ye ask Him." The point of asking is that you may get to know God better. "Delight thyself also in the Lord; and He shall give thee the desires of thine heart." Keep praying in order to get a perfect understanding of God Himself.

God the Father has given us this privilege so that we might know Him. In His high-priestly prayer in John 17 Jesus prayed:

> Father, the hour has come; glorify Thy Son, that the Son may glorify Thee, even as Thou gavest Him authority over all mankind, that to all whom Thou has given Him, He may give eternal life. And this is eternal life, that they may know Thee, the only true God, and Jesus Christ whom Thou hast sent (John 17:1-3).

Second Position

The Second Position of prayer is that of complete affirmation and commitment to God's kingdom and His will. It is the statement of a willing subject. If we say, "Thy kingdom come, Thy will be done," we are not only agreeing that God should accomplish this task and that others should join Him; we are giving Him our own allegiance. We are saying that this will be our own primary goal in life.

The Second Position in ballet is a preparatory position for moving out. Likewise, we become equipped before God through prayer to move out into the world so that God's kingdom and purpose will be fulfilled "on earth as it is in heaven." In prayer we are to receive our marching orders. Can you imagine a soldier not ever hearing the instructions for battle? If we are to work together with God to establish a kingdom, we must consult with the King. We need to have our briefing. We need to be in constant touch with the Commander. We cannot afford to do our own thing anymore. The Lord's work of establishing His kingdom in our hearts and of saving people out of the kingdom of darkness takes top priority.

Third Position

The Third Position of prayer is that of complete dependence upon the Lord for all our daily needs. Third Position in ballet is actually the easiest position to do correctly. That is why it is used regularly with beginners. The Third Position of prayer demonstrates our own weakness as human beings. We are not self- existing, self-sustaining little gods who can control every aspect of our own being or circumstances. We are so dependent upon God that our very breath comes from Him. He is our source, and when we recognize our complete dependence upon Him, He turns our weakness into His strength. This emphasis on our own personal weakness in the midst of the Lord's Prayer immediately follows the confession of relationship with the Father and the verbal commitment of loyalty to do His will. It is only as we confess our need of God and fully depend upon Him that we are made strong enough to do His will.

Fourth Position

The Fourth Position of prayer further emphasizes our weakness next to God's power and willingness to help us. Besides being physically dependent upon God, we find that we suffer from moral weakness. We have failed God and people, and we need forgiveness. This is the position of confession of sin, repentance, and restoration. Not only is this an admission of our guilt, but it is the answer to our weakness. If we try to hide our guilt from God and from ourselves, we keep ourselves from doing His will.

If we fail to seek God's forgiveness and if we fail to forgive others, we will also fail to enjoy the benefits of the prior positions of prayer. Although the relationship with the Father is still there, a wall of sin and guilt will stand in the way of communication. We will still be subjects of His kingdom, but we will be less able to do His will if we have not confessed known sin. Confession of sin is not for the purpose of feeling terrible and guilty; it is for restoration and new beginnings.

One might think that confessing sin and forgiving others should be easy, but it is not. It goes against the grain of the flesh. It requires a solid foundation of faith in God. It requires the two opposing forces, justice and mercy, to come together at the cross of Christ. Fourth Position in ballet is a difficult position to attain and maintain. The tendency is to lean more on one foot than the other—to be off-balance. That is exactly the problem we have with forgiveness: In order to confess sin and receive forgiveness, we must look at ourselves through God's truth and receive His mercy. In order to repent from sin, we must receive His mercy and choose to walk according to His truth. Furthermore, we have to keep in mind His part and our part. We confess; He forgives us. We receive His forgiveness and repent; He restores us and we obey. So often I have heard people get these things mixed up and say, "You must forgive yourself." No, it is not our part to forgive ourselves. That is God's place. What we really need to do is believe Him, gratefully accept His forgiveness, turn away from the sin, and go on to the next thing in life He has for us.

There is also a delicate balance in forgiving others. When others have sinned against us, our response may be to sin against them in our hearts. When we obtain God's grace to forgive others, we may also need to confess to God. Otherwise we may continue to be plagued with an undercurrent of blame, bitterness, or wrath. The best way to forgive others is to recognize how sinful we ourselves have been and how much worse we could be except for the grace of God. If we ever set ourselves up as better than others or more sinned against than sinning, we go out of balance. Those who retain hurt feelings for many years often do so because they have not recognized or confessed their own sins of both inner and outer response to the sins of others.

Fifth Position

The Fifth Position of prayer is much like the Third, just as the Fifth and Third positions in ballet are quite similar to each other. The Fifth Position is dependence on God to keep our attitudes, thoughts, words, and behavior from falling into sin. Here is complete dependence, not only for physical needs but for everything we do. This is moral and spiritual dependence. We may make New Year's resolutions, and we may make all sorts of promises to God and to ourselves, but unless we live in active dependence upon Him we will fail. Active dependence requires faith as well as choice: It depends upon faith in God rather than faith in self.

Active dependence on God also requires obedience. If by faith we choose to obey God through His enabling, we can accomplish His will. But here is the crux: We might choose to obey God for some selfish purpose, such as to have our own way to appear holy and righteous to others, to feel good about ourselves, or to become rich and famous. Dependence on God also requires uniting our will with His so that His will predominates. In so doing we give to God whatever rights we think we have.

Just as we must fully depend upon God for salvation, we must also fully depend upon Him for His life to work through us. Paul described his own absolute dependence on Jesus this way:

> I have been crucified with Christ; and it is no longer I who live, but Christ lives in me; and the life which I now live in the flesh I live by faith in the Son of God, who loved me and delivered Himself up for me (Galatians 2:20).

Then he asked the Galatians, "Are you so foolish? Having begun by the Spirit, are you now being perfected by the flesh?" (Galatians 3:3). He was trying to show them that their daily Christian walk could not be accomplished by their own ways or works or efforts any more than they could have saved themselves in the first place.

Such dependence implies putting God's plans and God's will above our own plans, enthusiasms, fears, and ambitions. I like the way a friend illustrated this for me. He compared walking in the Spirit to a train track with the rails running parallel in the same direction. And what might be the ties? Ties of God's love, ties of faith, ties of obedience. Both tracks work together as one.

What might a woman do with her mind? Lay it aside in mindless dependence? No! God gave each of us a brain to use, but now He asks us to use our intelligence to listen, learn, and communicate with Him. He has called us into a kind of partnership, not of equality (because He is God) but of friend. Jesus said to His disciples:

> You are My friends if you do what I command you. No longer do I call you slaves, for the slave does not know what his master is doing; but I have called you friends, for all things that I have heard from My Father I have made known to you (John 15:14, 15).

As brilliant as a woman might be, her mind is still very limited in comparison to her Lord's. She is still a little child in terms of knowledge, wisdom, and understanding. She needs God's perspective to know what is right and good in His sight. She must learn His knowledge rather than depend upon her own accumulation of facts. She must walk in dependence upon His wisdom rather than rely upon her own cleverness. And she must lean upon His understanding rather than promote her own opinions. Only in this position of prayer and humility does she discover the difference between the natural mind and the mind of Christ.

> A natural man does not accept the things of the Spirit of God, for they are foolishness to him, and he cannot understand them because they are spiritually appraised. But he who is spiritual appraises all things, yet he himself is appraised by no man. For who has known the mind of the Lord, that he should instruct Him? But we have the mind of Christ (1 Corinthians 2:14-16).

The highest position a human can take is that of kneeling at the cross of Christ.

The Lord's Prayer should make us humbly dependent upon our gracious heavenly Father. It opens the eyes of our hearts to the power, righteousness, and love of God. We gain confidence in Him as the One who has the power to work His will and His righteousness in us and through us. The Lord's Prayer gives us a glimpse of ourselves—dearly loved by God but totally dependent upon Him. As the majesty of God and the weakness of men come together in love, His strength is made perfect in our weakness. Where we are weak, He is strong. He is all in all to us. That is why the prayer ends by echoing the praise expressed in 1 Chronicles 29:11: "Thine, O Lord, is the greatness and the power and the glory."

Jesus calls us to pray because He knows that prayer is an absolute necessity. We cannot know God intimately without prayer. We cannot walk in the Spirit according to the ways of God unless we are in prayer. We cannot bear fruit in ministry except by prayer. Jesus prayed at every point along His journey. He prayed on the Mount of Transfiguration and He prayed in the valley. He prayed in Bethany so that Lazarus would come forth from the grave.

Jesus prayed for His disciples on the night of His betrayal. On the same night He urged His disciples to pray that they would not enter into temptation. While they slept, He knelt down and prayed the most agonizing prayer of His life. Through prayer He pre- pared for the cross, where He would bear the shame of the entire human race. On His knees in Gethsemane Jesus fought the battle in prayer.

"Father, if Thou art willing, remove this cup from Me; yet not My will but Thine be done."

Now an angel from heaven appeared to Him, strengthening Him. And being in agony He was praying very fervently; and His sweat became like drops of blood, falling down upon the ground.

And when He rose from prayer, He came to the disciples and found them sleeping from sorrow, and said to them, "Why are you sleeping? Rise and pray that you may not enter into temptation" (Luke 22:42-46).

Jesus won the battle in prayer and was prepared for the betrayal, the lies, the mocking, the scourging, and the crucifixion. The disciples, however, had not won the battle by praying. Jesus was the only One who was ready to meet every obstacle with firm resolve to do only the will of the Father.

Jesus has opened the way to the throne through His own blood sacrifice on the cross. He is our High Priest, seated next to the Father.

Let us therefore draw near with confidence to the throne of grace, that we may receive mercy and may find grace to help in time of need (Hebrews 4:16).

Not only has Jesus opened the way to the throne of grace, but He has given us the Holy Spirit to help us pray.

In the same way the Spirit also helps our weakness; for we do not know how to pray as we should, but the Spirit Himself intercedes for

us with groanings too deep for words; and He
who searches the hearts knows what the mind of
the Spirit is, because He intercedes for the saints
according to the will of God (Romans 8:26, 27).

God the Father hears our prayers, Jesus the Son intercedes for us while we are praying, and the Holy Spirit
helps us pray. With all this assistance and insistence, we
have no excuse. We cannot say that we don't know how,
because that doesn't matter. We cannot say we don't
have time, because God is the giver of time. We cannot
even say that we are too sinful, because forgiveness is
available.

If Christians do not pray, Satan wins the skirmish
hands down. The devil wins before the battle even begins.
No wonder he does all he can to keep us from praying!
We remain in our own weakness without prayer. We
depend upon our own measly resources without prayer.
We depend upon our own limited knowledge and wisdom without prayer. We remain in spiritual infancy without prayer.

The Bible is full of prayers of the saints, both in
the Old Testament and the New Testament. By reading
and praying those prayers we may discover aspects of
prayer that we have forgotten or perhaps never known.
For example, David's prayers reveal a broad spectrum
of emotions—frustration and peace, desperation and
confidence, fear and faith, hate and love, grief and joy
depression and praise. I have prayed through many of
the Psalms. Psalms 51 and 139 have been particularly
helpful. Besides the Psalms, one of my favorite prayers
is found in Ephesians 3:14-21. Another is in Colossians
1:9-12.

The best way to pray is simply this: Pray. Prayer is not a matter of eloquence; it is a matter of deciding to talk with God and then doing it. It is a matter of conversing with God every day even when nothing seems to be happening. It is a matter of simply obeying God. It is two-way communication in fellowship and love.

Devotional Exercise

1. Use the Lord's Prayer as a guideline for prayer. Make the prayer personal and pertinent to your own life. Fill in the details of each sentence.

2. In the following verses God says that He will do something and that there is a response for you to make. Take one of these verses and ask God for something specific that you need. Then depend upon God for it, no matter how small or great, and act according to His enabling.

Psalm 27:14 1

Corinthians 10:13

Galatians 5:22, 23

I John 1:8, 9

3. Pray the prayer of Colossians 1:9-12 for at least three other people as well as for yourself.

8

More Barre Work: Learning the Word

A serious ballet student strives to perform well even during the exercises at the *barre*. She is diligent because there is always room for improvement toward greater precision, strength, flexibility, and subtlety of expression. The technique must become second nature, so that each movement will be able to convey nuances of meaning. Because ballet is artistic communication rather than simply brilliant technique, the entire person is involved. The mind must be alert, the body under control, and the intent of the music and dance expressed.

The *tendu* generally follows the sequence of *pliés* at the *barre*. When the body is erect and the weight is correctly distributed over the supporting leg, the nonsupporting leg easily slides outward from a closed position (First, Third, or Fifth) to an open position (Second or Fourth). The extending leg retains straight firmness without awkward stiffness. As the leg moves outward, the foot extends and arches so that the heel leaves the floor while the tips of the toes touch the floor. The *tendu* is then completed by returning to the original position. The *tendu* gains its strength and beauty from correct body placement and from the way the foot relates to the floor.

The beginning of the *tendu* is the initial movement of many different steps in one direction or another, and the end of the *tendu* is the completion of many steps. If you ever see a ballet dancer whose foot is not perfectly pointed while off the floor, you will know that she needs more repetitions of the *tendu*. Besides beginning and ending everything with honoring God and thanking Him, a godly woman finds that everything she does must also begin and end with the Word of God.

Learning the Word of God is more than a casual reading. It is even more than study However, reading and study are basic requirements. How can we obey God if we do not read and study His Word? The enemy of our souls plies his craft to prevent us from getting into God's Word, because that is our source of knowledge, wisdom, and power to obey God and to resist temptation.

My introduction to disciplined Bible study was through Bible Study Fellowship, which is an international organization with study groups throughout the United States and in other parts of the world. A missionary, A Wetherell Johnson, began the work after having been incarcerated in a concentration camp in China during World War Two. She had found the Lord faithful during those bleak, horrible years. However, she noticed that not all Christians found inner strength in the Lord. Some continued in their faith, but others turned to despair. Some behaved as Christians, but others acted just like the unbelievers. She decided to find out what made the difference. And what she discovered was this: Those Christians who did not know the Word of God for themselves were the ones who managed very poorly under adverse conditions. They suffered the way the unbelievers suffered, without inner strength, without eternal hope, and without the love of God within their souls. On the other hand, those who had studied the Word of God for themselves found the strength they needed to endure the hardships in faith, hope, and love.

Because of this experience, she concluded that it is more important to help people study the Bible for themselves than to simply teach the Bible. She had learned through personal experience and observation that we must all be diligent students of the Word. Therefore, when she was asked to teach the Bible to a group of women in the United States, she determined that she would do it only if the women agreed to study the Bible on their own. She wrote questions to guide their personal study. Then, when the women gathered as a group, they shared what they had learned. After that Miss Johnson would fill in what they might have missed in their own study.

It may be easier to listen to an excellent Bible teacher than to study the Bible itself. However, the teacher will get far more out of the lesson than the listener, unless the listener prepares for the lesson as well. This in no way undermines the teaching and preaching of the Word of God. Instead, personal Bible study prepares our minds and hearts to actively respond to verbal presentations. Each believer has been given the responsibility to study the Word of God.

> Be diligent to present yourself approved to God
> as a workman who does not need to be ashamed,
> handling accurately the word of truth (2 Timothy
> 2:15).

Discipline of Bible study equips a woman of God for
every word she speaks and for every step she takes.

Read the Word

I wonder if we realize how blessed we are with the
privilege of knowing how to read, and especially how
blessed we are with the availability of Bibles! In earlier
days the very act of reading was held in high esteem.
The invention of the printing press set the stage for Bible
knowledge to spread throughout all classes of people.
No longer was it a hidden book, to be read and understood by only a few select persons.

Today, however, written literature is taken for
granted. It has dropped to third place, beneath television
and radio. Far less ability and attention are required to
watch an image on the television screen or to listen to
the radio or to audio cassettes than to read and study.
Reading takes effort; it is not a passive activity. Because
reading requires mental alertness and thinking, I believe
our society is the loser when it turns instead to more convenient forms of communication.

Reading activates and stimulates the mind differently
from television or radio. Although bits and pieces of reality may be imaged on television, we consider and evaluate truth through words. Weighing evidence and thinking through issues and concepts can be accomplished
only through language. Reliance on the image often

militates against such cerebral activities. Furthermore, people retain cognitive ideas far more by reading than through listening or viewing on television. The very act of reading requires mental activity and allows time to think, to ponder, to consider, to reread, to meditate, and to memorize.

The greatest excuse for not reading the Bible is that there is no time. Yet the average number of hours spent in front of the television screen astounds even the most informed observer. There is time to read the Bible! If there appears to be no time, it's time to set priorities. Deciding to spend 15 minutes every day reading the Bible is an act of the will. Doing it every day requires discipline.

Reading the Bible is different from any other kind of reading. The basic elements of reading words are the same, but the words in the Bible have been inspired by the Holy Spirit. They are more than simply words of men. Therefore the approach is different, just as your approach to reading a love letter would differ from reading a newspaper. The Author of the Book loves you, and He is there with you when you are reading the Bible. The approach should be one of anticipation, reverence, humility, and gratitude. Ask the Holy Spirit to illumine the Word to you. Read with expectation and read with a pen or pencil. Even though the Bible is the Holy Word of God, the paper itself is not sacred. Underlining, writing in the margins, and jotting down ideas or questions can be very helpful.

Rather than jumping around and reading a verse here and there, it is best to read through an entire book of the Bible. Then you have the sequence and the context for what is being said. You know where you have been and where you are going. It is one thing to look at a map and to point out the various cities and towns, but it is another thing to drive from one point to another.

There are also various ways of reading material: from skimming to reading aloud and from passive to active involvement. Some sections of Scripture, such as historical accounts and genealogies, may be read quickly, with the eye skimming across the page faster than one can mentally verbalize the words. Speed-reading is also a good way to pre-read a passage. In other words, to alert your mind to the basic ideas of a chapter, you may want to skim through it first and then read it more slowly and carefully the second time through. In this way you get the big picture first and then return to the details.

Many sections of Scripture require alert concentration; they cannot be read passively. Aggressive thinking is essential to grasp what is being said. In fact, certain sentences need to be read several times because so much is compacted into just a few words. Just as poetry cannot be comprehended through rapid or passive reading, the Bible requires careful, diligent reading.

Study the Word

Bible study involves more than reading. There are many methods of study, such as outlining, looking up reference material, cross-referencing verses, following themes and concepts throughout the Bible, memorizing, answering questions, writing notes, and so forth. Four questions to ask yourself while reading the Bible have been floating around the church for years: What does it say? What does it mean? What does it mean to me? What am I to do about it? They are excellent questions and provide an easy-to-remember method of Bible study. Furthermore, they involve both the mind and the behavior.

I tend to use a variety of methods. One approach I use in preparation for teaching employs one week to study one chapter. Before this in-depth study I read through the entire book at least once. I also read some general introduction to the book so that I have a historical and conceptual context for the book. Then I am ready to begin the process of one chapter per week. (Incidentally, during my "free" Bible reading time, I simply read through other books of the Bible so that I am not totally concentrated on one book of the Bible for weeks on end.)

On the first day I read through the chapter within the context of the book it is in. I jot down notes as to how it relates to the previous chapters and to the theme or intent of the book. I may reread some of the preceding chapters and skim the one that follows. Then I carefully read through the chapter again. Between the first time of study until the next, I think about it off and on during the day. I cogitate and meditate and pray. I consider various implications and recall other sections of Scripture that may deal with the same or related topics. The Lord starts to apply the Word to my own personal life for obedience and for change. The Bible cannot be understood without a personal response of obedience.

The next day I read the same chapter again, along with other sections of Scripture that may be related. From this day until the end of the week I use various study helps as they are needed, such as Bible dictionaries, maps, concordances, and handbooks. I may also read something about the customs of the day. Margin notes in the Bible are helpful for cross-referenced Scriptures on the same topic. However, I generally do not turn to commentaries until near the end of the week. I want to discover as much as I can with the help of the Holy Spirit before reading what other people have gleaned from the chapter. Writing down main ideas and outlining are helpful at this point. I also may write out a verse or two on a 3 x 5 card for memorizing during convenient times later in the day. And I may jot down personal applications. I continue to think about the chapter throughout the rest of the day In the meantime the Holy Spirit continues to prod me and help me to apply the truths in my own thinking, speaking, and behaving. On about the third or fourth day I write out study or discussion questions.

After spending most of the week digging the well for myself and drinking the water of the Word in my own life, I turn to the wells that others have dug and taste that water. At last it is time to read a commentary written by a reliable Bible scholar. That is when I discover how much I missed. The commentaries provide much additional information to incorporate into my own notes and outline.

Personal Bible study can be as intense and extensive as you want it to be. The above description may have put you to sleep or it may have seemed too tedious. However, you could take certain elements of the study and use them at different times. Even thinking about what you read in the Bible after you read it is an important element of study that can be done while driving or doing certain chores. Simply writing out important verses on 3 x 5 cards and then reading them at various times during the day gives opportunities for both thinking and obeying. I try to carry a few of them in my purse for those occasions when I'm standing in long lines, waiting in the car, or folding clean clothes. They can also be taped on mirrors, desks, and refrigerators.

Bible study groups that require diligence can serve to direct and stimulate personal study. I benefit from external motivation. If I am answerable to a group, I am more likely to do the work. If I am answerable only to myself, I can more easily procrastinate. Ballet dancers are the same way: They need the external motivation of the class as well as the instruction. Although they may practice for hours on their own, they still come together in a class to be answerable to an instructor. If you find that you need a class to help you discipline yourself in Bible study, by all means do so. But remember, the class is not for spoon-feeding but for making you hungry enough to feed yourself.

Use the Word

My cousin lived in Sweden for about a year after she graduated from college. She not only learned to speak the language, but she used it everywhere she went. When she returned to the States she intended to keep up her Swedish. But she didn't. She told me how embarrassed she was when she returned to Sweden years later, because she had lost her facility in the language.

Learning the Bible is similar. Unless we use the Word in our daily lives, we can lose it. Unless we use the Word to evaluate situations, thoughts, words, and actions, we will not retain enough of the Word to use it effectively. Although my cousin could still understand much of what was said, she had great difficulty putting sentences together to say what she wanted to say. The sounds and words were still familiar when she heard them, just as the words of the Bible may sound familiar. But when she tried to use them she was at a loss, just as when out-of-practice Christians fail to use the Word as their measuring stick and guide for living.

King David delighted in the Word of God. He found God's Word useful for restoring the soul, for giving wisdom and understanding, for guidance and warning, and for knowing God.

> The law of the Lord is perfect, restoring the soul;
> The testimony of the Lord is sure, making wise the simple.
> The precepts of the Lord are right, rejoicing the heart;
> The commandment of the Lord is pure, enlightening the eyes.
> The fear of the Lord is clean, enduring forever;
> The judgments of the Lord are true; they are righteous altogether.
> They are more desirable than gold, yes, than much fine gold;
> Sweeter also than honey and the drippings of the honeycomb.
> Moreover, by them Thy servant is warned;
> In keeping them there is great reward (Psalm 19:7-11).

The writer of Psalm 119 also loved and cherished the Word. He too found it extremely useful. It showed him the way of salvation and gave him hope. He also found understanding, wisdom, and guidance from the Word of God.

> May Thy lovingkindness also come to me, O Lord,
> Thy salvation according to Thy word;
> So shall I have an answer for him who reproaches me,
> For I trust in Thy word.
> And do not take the word of truth utterly out of my mouth,
> For I wait for Thine ordinances.
> So I will keep Thy law continually Forever and ever.
> And I will walk at liberty,
> For I seek Thy precepts.
> I will also speak of Thy testimonies before kings,
> And shall not be ashamed.
> And I shall delight in Thy commandments,
> Which I love.
> And I shall lift up my hands to Thy commandments,
> Which I love;
> And I will meditate on Thy statutes (Psalm 119:41-48).

The writer continues for a total of 176 verses with such words as:

Thy commandments make me wiser than my enemies,

For they are ever mine.

I have more insight than all my teachers,

For Thy testimonies are my meditation.

I understand more than the aged,

Because I have observed Thy precepts. . . .

Thy word is a lamp to my feet,

And a light to my path (Psalm 119:98-100,105).

We need to use the Word of God to evaluate what we see around us and on television; what we hear from teachers, preachers, friends, and relatives; and what we read in books, magazines, and newspapers. We need to use the Word to discern truth from error. Indeed, we must use the Word even to evaluate preaching and teaching of the Word to be sure that the leaven of error has not penetrated the sermon or teaching. Jesus warned about the leaven of the Pharisees, who mixed the traditions and opinions of men with the true Word of God. False teaching hides itself in such a way that those who do not know the Word for themselves can be easily fooled.

Paul was confronted with all kinds of reactions to his preaching and teaching. Some people eagerly accepted his words, but others tried to stone him. However, the listeners in Berea were called "noble-minded" because "they received the word with great eagerness, examining the Scriptures daily, to see whether these things were so" (Acts 17:11). Their enthusiasm, however, did not prevent them from checking everything with Scripture. A pastor who truly shepherds his people will desire that they eagerly receive the Word. He will also encourage them to "examine the Scriptures daily" to evaluate even his own preaching. On the other hand, those teachers who love their own knowledge more than the Word of God will not tolerate anyone using the Word of God to question what they teach.

A well-known speaker complained about people who wanted him to substantiate his teachings with Scripture. That is a sad commentary on our day, but it is an admonition for us to be alert and to know the Word of God well enough to discern what is true and what is false. It is no longer an option—we must know and become skilled at using the Word of God as the light of truth in these days of widespread deception.

Besides being a tool of discernment, the Word of God is extremely useful for knowledge, wisdom, and guidance for our daily lives. It is a perfect standard for thinking, speaking, and acting. The Word of God is also a sword of the Spirit by which to resist temptation. The Bible is our most useful book and most effective tool for living. It is more useful than any man-made instrument or machine. It is more useful than any knowledge or wisdom devised by humans. The Word of God gives us more accurate knowledge about the way to live than any philosophy or psychology could ever hope to find.

A ballet dancer must exercise her knowledge of ballet every day in order to maintain her level of expertise. Even a few days away from the *barre* will lessen her ability to perform up to standard. To keep the Word useful to us, we need to keep using it for learning, evaluating, and correcting our own attitudes, thoughts, words, and actions. We also need to keep on using it to evaluate what we see, hear, and read.

Devotional Exercise

1. Read through a book of the Bible, such as Ephesians.

2. Study one chapter in depth for one week.

    a. Read the chapter every day and think about it throughout the day

    b. Look up important words in a Bible dictionary. You may also wish to look up information about locations and customs in an atlas and/or handbook.

    c. Outline the chapter and try to condense the content into one sentence.

    d. Find other Scripture passages that relate to the one you are reading. Margin notes are helpful for this, or you can look up key words in a concordance.

    e. Write out personal applications from this chapter, de- scribing how you might apply them to your own life.

9

Correction: Being a Disciple

Throughout a dancer's development, the teacher plays an extremely important role. The teacher cultivates the students by including those movements at the barre which the students most need to practice. She instructs and demonstrates. She combines various movements, according to the technical level of the group, to increase both mental and physical agility. The instructor carefully watches each dancer and makes both group and individual corrections. She is constantly examining and correcting for the sake of each student's technical and artistic development.

The Christian woman also has a Teacher who instructs, demonstrates, examines, and corrects. The Lord Himself instructs through His Word and through His Holy Spirit indwelling the believer. The Lord Jesus demonstrated how each one of us is to live by faith, hope, and love. He demonstrated every step in the Christian walk, and the Holy Spirit applies that demonstration to each present possibility for thinking, speaking, acting, and reacting. The Lord also examines us through His Word and through His Holy Spirit.

> The word of God is living and active and sharper than any two-edged sword, and piercing as far as the division of soul and spirit, of both joints and marrow, and able to judge the thoughts and intentions of the heart. And there is no creature hidden from His sight, but all things are open and laid bare to the eyes of Him with whom we have to do (Hebrews 4:12, 13).

What a privilege to be so carefully examined by God! Although the world would hide from His presence, every Christian should desire to be examined by the Lord, because He examines us in order to correct us in love. He examines to restore and renew. He examines to reveal and supply what each of us needs in order to become more like Jesus. He examines to cause each of us to walk in His way. King David yearned for this examination as he prayed:

> Search me, 0 God, and know my heart; Try me and know my anxious thoughts; And see if there be any hurtful way in me, And lead me in the everlasting way (Psalm 139:23, 24).

We have a Teacher we can trust. He does not simply criticize for the sake of criticism. He does not condemn His children. Rather, He convicts of sin in order to cleanse and restore. He is making something greater than ballerinas—He is making saints into the image of Christ! He is making pure vessels of His love and righteousness.

The natural man does not like correction. Today everyone cries out for affirmation. We crave compliments and praise. We would rather receive a word of commendation than a word of correction. We want to hear positive statements about ourselves. And yet, in His love, which perfectly combines grace and truth, the Lord corrects us. Too often we have equated love with affirmation rather than with correction. We have heard love in compliments and praise, but not in criticism. However, both a wise ballet dancer and a wise Christian recognize the value of the negative as well as the positive. King Solomon shared the wisdom that God gave him about how to receive correction:

> Whoever loves discipline loves knowledge, But he who hates reproof is stupid (Proverbs 12:1).

> A wise son accepts his father's discipline, But a scoffer does not listen to rebuke (Proverbs 13:1).

> He who corrects a scoffer gets dishonor for himself, And he who reproves a wicked man gets insults for himself. Do not reprove a scoffer, lest he hate you, Reprove a wise man, and he will love you. Give instruction to a wise man, and he will be still wiser, Teach a righteous man, and he will increase his learning (Proverbs 9:7-9).

> He whose ear listens to the life-giving reproof will dwell among the wise. He who neglects discipline despises himself, But he who listens to reproof acquires understanding. The fear of the

Lord is the instruction for wisdom, And before honor comes humility (Proverbs 15:31-33).

Correction from the Lord may not be pleasant for the moment, but the results are great. It may seem easier to justify ourselves and refuse to face sin in our lives, but acceptance of correction actually makes future actions easier. A dancer may refuse correction and forever struggle with the same hindrances.

Our daughter Margot studied flute for many years. She reached a point at which her instructor told her that if she were to progress any further she would have to learn how to use her fingers differently. The change was not an easy one. It was almost like starting out all over again with a brand new technique. Not only did she have to learn a new way, but she had to unlearn the old. Each time she picked up her flute, she had to deliberately choose the new way until she had developed the new habit of fingering. This is like correction in the Christian walk. It may seem much easier to think, speak, and act according to the old patterns, but there will be no progress unless the change is made deliberately—not once, not twice, but over and over again.

Sometimes things may seem to get worse for awhile rather than better. My *arabesque* deteriorated greatly for a period of time while I was unlearning a bad habit. I had been inadvertently raising my hip too high in order to get my leg up higher. This made the line of the *arabesque* awkward and actually limited how high I would eventually be able to lift my leg. The *arabesque* could not improve until I made the correction. However, while I worked on body alignment and hip placement during the *arabesque*, I could not raise my leg as high as I had before. An untrained observer would certainly have thought that the arabesque was worse, but my teacher knew better. She continued to encourage the correct placement of the hip rather than the height of the leg.

The same thing often happens when we begin to replace old habits. For awhile things may seem to get worse before they get better. This also happens in relationships. If I begin to treat someone differently from before, he may have to learn to relate to me in new ways as well. Also, I believe that things may seem worse during the early stages of developing godly habits because we are in a spiritual battle.

Even though change may be difficult, the Lord's correction brings with it His promise to work in us. As we choose to change according to His plan, He enables us to do so. The Lord's correction brings hope rather than discouragement or despair, because He is able to do what He has promised. I love the truth of the benediction of the epistle to the Hebrews.

> Now the God of peace, who brought up from the dead the great Shepherd of the sheep through the blood of the eternal covenant, even Jesus our Lord, equip you in every good thing to do His will, working in us that which is pleasing in His sight, through Jesus Christ, to whom be the glory forever and ever. Amen (Hebrews 13:20,21).

God is both willing and able to do this, but He asks for our cooperation.

The first way we cooperate with God's correction is by agreeing with Him. That is what confession really is. When He points out sin or error, we agree that He is right. The second step is to choose to turn away from sin—that is, to stop sinning. In turning away from sin we leave it behind us by receiving God's forgiveness. He wipes away the sin so that it will not stand between Himself and us. And, third, we begin again. We look to God to show us the right way and to enable us to do His will.

Just as in a ballet class the teacher may give the same correction over and over again to a person who is learning new habits, so the Lord is patient to give the same correction over and over again. His forgiveness, cleansing, and renewing are available each time.

> If we confess our sins, He is faithful and righteous to forgive us our sins and to cleanse us from all unrighteousness (I John 1:9).

I count on this promise. I need it daily because God is also faithful to correct me.

The amount of correction does not indicate where a person is along the way of becoming like Jesus. Correction merely indicates that change is necessary. An advanced ballet student may receive more correction than a beginner, because the teacher is then able to work on details of performance rather than on basic movements. Therefore we must never be discouraged. We are on our way to glory as long as He continues to correct us.

The most devastating place for a ballet student to be is beyond correction. Some students will not receive correction, and therefore the teacher leaves them alone. The same thing happens to people who will not receive correction from the Lord. He leaves them to their own devices. Those who will not hear from the Lord will no longer be able to hear Him. This happened to Israel over and over again, so much so that God told Isaiah that the people would not heed his words. Look at what happened to those who would not honor God as God but chose to set themselves up as little gods:

> Professing to be wise, they became fools, and exchanged the glory of the incorruptible God for an image in the form of corruptible man.... Therefore God gave them over in the lusts of their hearts to impurity that their bodies might be dishonored among them. For they exchanged the truth of God for a lie, and worshiped and served the creature rather than the Creator, who is blessed forever. Amen. For this reason God gave them over to degrading passions.... (Romans 1:22-26).

Correction is a blessing. God corrects us because He loves us.

> My son, do not regard lightly the discipline of the Lord, nor faint when you are reproved by Him; For those whom the Lord loves He disciplines, and He scourges every son whom He receives....
>
> All discipline for the moment seems not to be joyful, but sorrowful; yet to those who have been trained by it, afterwards it yields the peaceful fruit of righteousness (Hebrews 12:5, 6, 11).

God's discipline is based upon truth and righteousness and is motivated by His love. It is for the purpose of fruit-bearing. Every difficult circumstance in a believer s life holds in it the possibility of training and discipline by the Lord. He wastes nothing that we will allow Him to use in our lives—no sorrow, no loss, no grief, no pain. All can be used to make us like Jesus, if we will yield ourselves to Him and ask Him to reveal what He desires to accomplish in our lives.

All of the students in a ballet class need similar instruction and correction. However, a superior instructor is very much in tune with each dancer's development. She corrects each student somewhat differently, both in manner and in the choice of correction. Two dancers may look the same to an untrained eye, but they will receive quite different correction. For instance, during the *frappes*, which are very rapid beats of one foot at the ankle of the other, the teacher may correct the posture of one dancer, the turnout of another, the angle of the foot of another, and the rhythm of another.

The Lord works with us both as a body of believers and as unique individuals. Although He is conforming all of us to the image of Christ, He works on different aspects of faith, hope, and love within our various circumstances and according to our own peculiarities. He molds and shapes us according to His design and according to His familiarity with the clay.

Furthermore, God does not work on all areas of change at the same time. He is selective. If a ballet teacher were to correct every detail, a dancer could become confused and discouraged. The demands would overwhelm her. Likewise we could become over- whelmed if God were to work on every problem at once. Our precious Lord is specific in His correction and does not give us too much at the same time. If we do become overwhelmed with too many things to change all at once, we need to check to see what God is working on. When the Holy Spirit corrects or convicts us of sin, He is specific and He is there to administer the Father's forgiveness and Jesus' cleansing. The Holy Spirit offers hope. He has a solution which can be found in God's Word. He has a better way to show us and He helps us to change.

Correction occurs in three general categories: faith, hope, and love. If faith has been replaced by doubt or fear, or if faith has been placed in something or someone other than God Himself, the basis of the correction will be to restore faith in God within the present attitude, thought, word, action, and circumstance. If hope has been replaced by false confidence in temporary things— such as a career, upward mobility, money, health, or personal power—or by a sense of hopelessness and despair, then the basis of the correction will be to restore hope in God. If the love relationship with God has been overshadowed by love of anything or anyone more than love for God, or if there is any question concerning how much God loves the believer, then the basis of the correction will be to renew the love.

Some of the saddest words were spoken to the church in Ephesus. After commending them for good deeds and perseverance, the Lord said, "But I have this against you, that you have left your first love" (Revelation 2:4). The Lord keeps special watch on faith, hope, and love, because it is from these three aspects of relationship with Him that He works in us and through us. That is why Satan tempted Eve in these areas—to pull her away from God so that he could control the world. He undermined the Word of God with his crafty mixture of truth and lie. He thus tempted Eve to believe his words instead of

God's Word and to put her faith in the fruit and in herself rather than in God alone. He undermined her hope for her future with God by giving her a false hope: to never die and to be like God through her own independent means, rather than in complete dependence upon God to lead her and to show her the way. The walk is away from God whenever hope is placed outside of Him alone. And finally, Satan implied that God did not really love Eve because He was withholding good from her. So Eve turned away from God and placed her faith, hope, and love in lies, in things, in herself—in everything but God.

The Holy Spirit uses the Word to reveal to us what needs to be corrected. There are many passages which the Holy Spirit will use during various times in our life. One passage that has been extremely helpful to me is Philippians 4:6, 7:

> Be anxious for nothing, but in everything by prayer and supplication with thanksgiving let your requests be made known to God. And the peace of God, which surpasses all comprehension, shall guard your hearts and your minds in Christ Jesus.

Here is a correction that I have to make repeatedly As soon as something seems to be awry, I tend to worry. That is my natural response in the flesh. When the Teacher reproves me, there are several responses I can make: I can ignore Him, or I can justify my anxious thoughts by telling Him how bad things are, or I can try to get rid of them through sheer willpower—through self-effort. I can even feel guilty and condemned for being anxious. And I can tell myself that I can't help it. On the other hand, I can turn to my Lord and choose to believe Him.

I can turn to Him and find the hope I need in Him. I can turn to Him in love and receive His love in my moment of need.

The Word of God is specific regarding anxiety. If His directions are followed His way, they will work. However, many people try to follow these words like a formula in such a way as to be relying on self rather than on God. Any attempt at obeying God without relying upon Him will fall short of His solutions and plans. Sometimes only part of God's directions are followed, or they are followed with an attitude of unbelief. Faith is a prerequisite for obeying God's Word in God's way.

The first part of the command is to be anxious about nothing. This does not mean that I must simply stop being anxious. Nor does it mean that I don't do anything about the situation that has stimulated the anxious thoughts. Within the same sentence is the first replacement for anxiety: "But in everything by prayer and supplication with thanksgiving let your requests be made known to God." Notice that four words are used in the instruction: *prayer*, *supplication*, *thanksgiving*, and *requests*.

If in prayer I keep my mind on the very thing I'm anxious about, I'll probably slip into what I call "pray-worry," which is simply worrying to God rather than praying in faith. On the other hand, if I focus on God rather than on the problem, I will gain His perspective. If the focus is right, the problem looks smaller than God. This is not to deny the problem or to avoid doing something about it. Rather, as soon as I come into God's presence with the problem I become ready to receive His instructions and help.

Someone once said that prayer doesn't simply change things; prayer changes people. And the person who is usually changed is the person who is praying. Then, as the problem is presented to the Father in faith, humility, and gratitude, the first answer is inner peace: "The peace of God, which surpasses all comprehension, shall guard your hearts and your minds in Christ Jesus." What fantastic peace! It is peace that reaches the depths of the inner person and guards the mind. That sounds like the answer to anxiety doesn't it? Well, it's just the first part of the answer. What if the anxiety has been stimulated by real circumstances? Then more has to be done. God gives peace so that we can obey Him in what He intends to do about the situation.

Besides being an excellent checklist for our thought life, Philippians 4:8 is also God's method for problem-solving.

> Finally brethren, whatever is true, whatever is honorable, whatever is right, whatever is pure, whatever is lovely, whatever is of good repute, if there is any excellence and if anything worthy of praise, let your mind dwell on these things.

What a list for checking options! As we consider what God would have us do in any given situation, we can let our minds "dwell on these things." This list does not eliminate the negative, as some people think. There is no place for ignoring the facts, no matter how ugly they are. No, this list begins with truth. We must face truth from God's perspective. Then our own actions must meet the standards that follow. They must be honorable, right, pure, and even lovely.

When anxious thoughts come, prayer is the first step. Then God's peace enables us to think clearly in order to solve the problem according to His righteousness. Finally we are to act according to the examples that God has given us in His Word. Paul wrote:

> The things you have learned and received and heard and seen in me, practice these things; and the God of peace shall be with you (Philippians 4:9).

The Teacher points out anxiety. The correction comes through prayer and through thinking and acting His way. Every reproof brings with it a correction, a solution, and a change.

Because of the gracious correction of the Lord and because of the enabling of the Holy Spirit, I found myself following His design for problem solving during a few hectic hours in Munich. I was standing on a platform in the train station, which sounded like a monstrous echo chamber as the trains lumbered in. I had to shout above the din, and every word I said was of utmost importance. I was responsible for getting 180 students and teachers to Paris. In my hand I held 180 tickets for seats scattered among a long number of cars. I shouted directions and handed out the tickets one by one. The train squealed to a stop. In a great scurry all my tourists disappeared among the crowd. I wouldn't know until the next morning that each person made it.

The tour had not been at all the way I had expected it to be. Martin and I were only supposed to have been helping with the tour while learning the ropes. However, the owner had suddenly decided to return to the States and leave the group in our care. By the end of the first week I had been ready to pack my bags and go home. But then God gave me a totally different perspective, so that by the time I was on the Munich platform I was working hand in hand with Jesus. Martin had preceded us to Paris to arrange for housing, but Jesus was with me.

How did I manage to have God's perspective on the platform in Munich? How did I shift from my point of view to His? I had come to an end of wanting my own way on that trip. God in His mercy, grace, and wisdom showed me that tour was not for my pleasure. I was there to serve. I was a servant. And, above all, I was His servant. The release was astonishing. Since I was merely His servant, He was in charge. God had made that correction in a small room in Florence. He had changed my perspective so that by the time I was in Munich I could see that He was in charge even in the midst of the confusion.

I could have wasted emotional energy complaining about the terrible travel plans that had been provided for the trip, but God had given me His perspective. Instead, I used my energy to salvage what we had—180 scattered seats and 180 exhausted students. I was working with God even though I looked pretty ridiculous—running up and down and shouting directions. I had His peace and His authority. I had my part to do and He had His. On the Munich platform I tasted what it was like to be anxious for nothing in spite of the circumstances. God did His part wonderfully. Every student arrived safely in Paris on time with every piece of luggage!

Getting God's perspective is not an instant makeover. Nor is it like putting on rose-colored glasses. It's more like getting to know someone so well that you know his likes and dislikes. It takes time, but it's worth it. I was learning to ask myself, "How does Jesus see this situation? What would He do if He were me? What can He do in me and through me, since He is living in me?" I was learning the joy that comes from God's correction.

Once the correction is made at the barre during one class, the student and teacher work together to maintain the correction during subsequent classes. The change is meant to become a habit. If the teacher has corrected the direction and manner in which the knees are to be held in the five ballet positions and the student does not continue to make the correction on her own, serious knee problems can develop and prevent further training. When God shows us a new pattern of response to anxiety, He means for us to continue following the new pattern until it becomes a habit. Doing it right once may be great for the moment, but God wants the new pattern of response to be permanent. We become true disciples of the Lord as we receive His discipline and then continue in that discipline.

The student assimilates the correction given at the *barre* and continues to correct herself. This is not a totally independent act because the corrections she is making are usually those that the teacher has previously given her: "Pull up around the center as you prepare for the *pirouette*.... Distribute your weight evenly between both feet before you *relevé* and turn.... Don't poke your head forward.... Keep your eye on your spot longer and then snap your head quickly.... Land with a softer *plié*." A teacher cannot say everything all at once. The student must remember the directions and the corrections. The same is true of a person who is walking with God. He has even given us the Holy Spirit to help us remember His directions and corrections.

Corrections never end, even for a prima ballerina. Corrections of artistic expression follow the years of corrections in technique. They become more refined and subtle as the choreographer guides her into the nuances of the role she is dancing. How well she perceives his instructions and how well she is able to interpret and express his intentions will make the difference between being an artist or merely a technician.

Our Lord not only guides us in godly living as far as doing what is right and good; He has called us to be His representatives, to express His love in attitude and action, in thought and word. Therefore, expect the training to continue. Expect the discipline, the reproof, and the correction, because He is molding us into creatures who will one day reflect the perfection of our Lord Jesus Christ.

Devotional Exercise

1. Read Hebrews 12 as an encouragement to persevere in the Christian life. What are the advantages of being disciplined by the Lord? What is the main reason for His discipline?

2. Hebrews 13 includes a long list of godly attitudes and actions. As you read through the list, allow the Lord to point out one verse for you to obey with His enabling. Write down the verse and the application to your life.

3. Read Romans 8. What is the difference between obeying according to self-effort and obeying by

cooperating with the indwelling Holy Spirit? Look at your answer to question 2. How do you plan to obey?

10

Discipline: Thoughts and Actions

After a strenuous *barre*, the dancers are ready to move to the center. The atmosphere of precision and unison disintegrates as each dancer "recovers" by stretching or massaging tight muscles or wipes down with a towel. Some will cluster around the resin box to add a bit of stickiness to the bottoms of the slippers to avoid slipping during the center work. Almost as quick as the scattering is the recollecting and reforming. The dancers space themselves and resume the ballet stance, ready for even more demanding work than at the *barre*.

The center work begins with some of the same exercises as at the *barre—demi* and *grand pliés, tendus, ronds de jambes, arabesques*—combined in various forms and sequences. Whereas the *barre* provided the basic learning and practicing place for isolated movements and simple combinations, the center is like everyday life, where Bible knowledge is practiced in a multitude of circumstances. It is the place where our Christianity is challenged, tested, and lived.

Just as dancers learn only by actually doing what is taught, so Christians learn only by doing. Jesus gave this analogy:

> Everyone who hears these words of Mine and acts upon them may be compared to a wise man who built his house upon the rock. And the rain descended, and the floods came, and the winds blew, and burst against that house; and yet it did not fall, for it had been founded upon the rock.
>
> And everyone who hears these words of Mine and does not act upon them will be like a foolish man who built his house upon the sand. And the rain descended, and the floods came, and the winds blew, and burst against that house; and it fell, and great was its fall (Matthew 7:24-27).

In a multitude of combinations, the woman of God practices faith, hope, and love. Rather than being her own boss, she is under the Lord's rulership. Through submission and cooperation, she gives the indwelling Holy Spirit preeminence. She uses her mind to know God and to learn His will. She then uses her own will to do what is right. She also brings her emotions into harmony with God's will through choosing His thoughts and His actions. In this way she becomes a vessel of honor to the Lord.

Combinations of movements involve both the inner and the outer life. As one aspect of a person's life is brought into harmony with the will of God, other facets will be influenced and changed. For instance, godly choices and actions lead to godly emotions and attitudes. C. S. Lewis stated this principle very well in his book *Mere Christianity*:

> Do not waste time bothering whether you love your neighbour; act as if you did. As soon as we do this we find one of the great secrets. When you are behaving as if you loved someone, you will presently come to love him.

Faith, hope, and love are intrinsically joined together. Thoughts and actions also work together. Nevertheless, each will be emphasized along the way, just as each part of a *pirouette* may be isolated for the sake of correction and perfection. The preparation for a *pirouette* will partly determine the balance, speed, and number of revolutions of the actual *pirouette*. Thus the dancer may practice the preparation over and over again, both with and without the *pirouette*. Likewise, a godly woman may practice faith in her thinking in preparation for exercising faith in her speaking and acting.

Have you ever noticed how much time you spend thinking? Thoughts reflect a person's faith, hope, and love. The inner life affects every facet of our being.

> Watch over your heart with all diligence, For from it flow the springs of life (Proverbs 4:23).

Words and behavior reveal the inner person: the inner thoughts, motivations, and attitudes.

I recall approaching the high gray walls of a prison. Towers housing fully armed guards jutted up at regular intervals. We climbed the stone stairs and entered the reception area. Heavy bars loomed in front of us. As we walked toward iron-barred gates, they slid open. We stepped through and they slammed shut. The slam echoed again and again as if to emphasize utter finality.

Just a few of us were crowded into the heavily guarded room. After a few moments the bars in front of us slid apart and we entered the next human cage. Again the doors slammed behind us and again the sounds repeated throughout the chamber. We waited. Another set of bars opened into yet another caged area. We stumbled ahead and again the gate slammed behind us. As the final set of bars opened their jaws, we stepped into a long corridor. On our right we could see visitors seated on stools and speaking through bars. We proceeded further. As we were led into the depths of the building, we passed cell blocks with their ponderous doors and tiers of cells. At last we reached our destination—a dingy, half-lit auditorium.

My cousin and I went up to the balcony and sat down. She was perfectly relaxed, for she had been there many times before. But the feeling of being locked in and never getting out enveloped me. We looked down as men filed into the rows on the main floor. Guards patrolled the aisles while the lights dimmed further and the film began. My uncle was the superintendent of the men's reformatory. We had simply come to the auditorium to see a movie. Nevertheless, with the help of a 13-year-old's imagination, I tasted a bitter morsel of what it must feel like to live in prison.

There are all kinds of prisons, some more heavily secured than others, some with more restrictions, some with more cruelty, and some with unbearable punishment. But not all prisons have metal bars. Not all prisons occupy a space of land and surround themselves with heavy walls and armed guards. Some of the worst prisons are invisible to the human eye, but are nevertheless experienced in the cruelest ways. They are prisons of fear, bitterness, hatred, frustration, boredom, disappointment, depression, unbelief, and pride.

How people get into those kinds of prisons has been speculated throughout the centuries; philosophies, psychologies, and religions all attempt to explain how and why But the Bible reveals God's perspective on the matter of how and why people get into such internal prisons, and it also explains how to get out. The Bible says that all of us have sinned. Not only have we sinned in our own actions, but we have sinned in our response to the sins of other people. Although some of us may feel like the victims of other people's sins, internal prisons are built with stone blocks of our own making rather than by those that other people may hurl against us. For example the prison of bitterness is not built by the person who may have stimulated the response of bitterness; it is built by the person who persists in bitter thinking.

Once inside such a prison, how do the inmates get out? Where are the doors? Who has the key to unlock the doors? Who can grant the pardon, the release? Who can lead them out? Isaiah looked at the wayward people of God and looked forward to the One who would set prisoners free. He prophesied:

> The Spirit of the Lord is upon me, Because the Lord has anointed me To bring good news to the afflicted; He has sent me to bind up the brokenhearted, To proclaim liberty to captives

> And freedom to prisoners; To proclaim the
> favorable year of the Lord, And the day of
> vengeance of our God; To comfort all who mourn,
> To grant those who mourn in Zion, Giving them
> a garland instead of ashes, The oil of gladness
> instead of mourning, The mantle of praise instead
> of a spirit of fainting. So they will be called oaks
> of righteousness, The planting of the Lord, That
> He may be glorified (Isaiah 61:1-3).

When Jesus spoke to the crowd in Nazareth, He said that He was the One prophesied. And He has done what He promised, for He purchased the key on the cross and opens the door to new life. Jesus not only sets prisoners free; He renews them in their minds. He washes away the sin of the inner life as well as the sins committed outwardly He clothes believers with His righteousness and truth.

Jesus gives people a different way to think. Throughout the Christian walk, Jesus continues to transform believers by renewing their minds. In this renewal, He asks them to believe Him and His Word above their own thoughts and feelings. The choice to love and trust Him in obedience enables Christians to overcome the bondage of erroneous patterns of thinking. Such a choice frees them from being controlled by ungodly thoughts and feelings.

From the point of salvation onward, the Lord asks believers to give themselves to Him so that He can work His perfect will in them. Paul urged:

> Do not be conformed to this world, but be
> transformed by the renewing of your mind, that

you may prove what the will of God is, that which is good and acceptable and perfect (Romans 12:2).

The external evidence of the will of God in a person's life begins in the mind, in attitudes and thoughts. Jesus taught:

> . . . the mouth speaks out of that which fills the heart. The good man out of his good treasure brings forth what is good; and the evil man out of his evil treasure brings forth what is evil (Matthew 12:34, 35).

What is inside eventually comes out. Therefore we need to be putting good things into our inner treasure house. We need to feed our minds with things which will stimulate godly thoughts and attitudes. Reading and meditating on God's Word provide opportunities for His truth to renew the mind. For example, we can renew our mind by reading Psalm 138. This psalm reminds us that we exercise volition as to what we do with our minds, our mouths, and our hands. Furthermore, the psalm reminds us of God's lovingkindness, truth, faithfulness, and active involvement in our lives.

> I will give Thee thanks with all my heart; I will sing praises to Thee before the gods. I will bow down toward Thy holy temple, And give thanks to Thy name For Thy lovingkindness and Thy truth; For Thou hast magnified Thy word According to all Thy name (Psalm 138:1, 2).

It takes just a few minutes to read the psalm several times. It is good for the soul. It supplies food for thought.

Thinking about what the psalmist has written helps each reader to digest and assimilate the truth. Meditating on the psalm throughout the day brings an increase in richness of understanding and application.

On the other hand, we can choose to fill our minds with junk food—romance novels, television, magazines, and gossip. The good food of the Word of God strengthens the inner man and produces good fruit. The junk food feeds dissatisfaction, fear, doubt, hostility, bitterness, anger, depression, and anxiety. Furthermore, the junk food weakens our ability to say and do what is pleasing to God.

Even those who have convinced themselves that they cannot control their thoughts do make a choice. They may choose carelessly and tolerate whatever pops into their minds. Perhaps they have developed passive habits of thinking so that it feels as though their thinking has a "mind of its own." Or perhaps they allow their emotions to control their thinking and acting. Some people follow old patterns of erroneous thinking rather than choosing to think according to the indwelling presence of the Holy Spirit. Those who insist that they cannot change actually refuse to give up the old familiar ways, no matter how erroneous and destructive they are.

For the Christian, thinking should not be divorced from relationship to God. The Bible makes it very clear that we are responsible for our thought life. Although thoughts may seem to come without our bidding, it is up to us whether or not they stay In his devotional, *My Utmost/or His Highest*, Oswald Chambers wrote about the Christian's responsibility for his thinking.

I have to construct with patience the way of thinking that is exactly in accordance with my Lord. God will not make me think like Jesus, I have to do it myself; I have to bring every thought into captivity to the obedience of Christ. "Abide in Me"—in intellectual matters, in money matters, in every one of the matters that make human life what it is.

Too often we fail to do God's will in our outer actions because we have not brought our inner thoughts under submission to Him. Jesus even went so far as to point out the sinful nature of certain thoughts in relation to sinful acts. Doubt and fear begin in the mind. Lust begins in the mind. Temptation occurs in the mind, and if we entertain sinful thoughts, we are engaging in sin before we act it out. One day a woman described the fear she encountered every time her son was out late at night. She would imagine the worst kinds of accidents with all the accompanying details of sight and sound. The imagined accident was not just a flash of thought, but developed into an entire scenario of grief and gore. This woman needed to feed her mind on the Word of God rather than the late-night movies and newscasts. Furthermore, she needed to learn to bring every thought into submission to Jesus. She did not realize that she had a real and valid choice regarding her thinking. Although an initial thought may intrude upon our minds, we can choose what to do with it.

A Christian woman who had endured a great deal of dental work throughout her childhood, including three sessions of extensive dental surgery was gripped by fear whenever she sat in a dental chair. She knew that the fear was ridiculous, especially when she was just having her teeth cleaned. Nevertheless, she could feel the fear creep over her entire body, with her sweaty hands, pounding heart, and tense muscles all on red alert.

One day while she was having her teeth cleaned, the Holy Spirit convicted her of her lack of faith and trust. What kind of witness was this to a renewed life in Jesus? How could there still be this fear after she had come into a personal relationship with Jesus and been crucified with Christ and no longer had to fear what man could do to her? But there it was, as intense as ever. She began to pray. Instead of concentrating on the fear and instead of even trying to conquer the fear, she began to fill her mind with the truth of God's love and care.

Every time she went to the dentist over a period of about a year-and-a-half, she filled her mind with the truth of God while she was in the dental chair. She followed the promise and admonition of Isaiah 26:3, 4:

> Thou wilt keep him in perfect peace whose mind is stayed on thee, because he trusteth in thee. Trust ye in the Lord forever, for in the Lord Jehovah is everlasting strength (KJV).

After the first few sessions she realized that her mind was no longer gripped with fear. However, her body retained all the previous symptoms. Finally, one day she noticed that her body was relaxed and that the fear was gone. She was free. God had worked a miracle in her, and she had cooperated by choosing to put His truth above her feelings.

Many of us continue as prisoners of our own emotions, because we do not understand that we can choose to put the truth of God above the emotion. When we elevate God's truth above our own reasoning and above our emotions, we find release. However, we need to persist. We need to continue to choose until God's Word takes precedence over the emotions so as to bring them in harmony with His truth. When we choose to trust and obey God more than our feelings, and when we believe God's Word more than our own thoughts, we allow God to perform His work of renewing our mind. The feelings and thoughts may scream and shout even after we put them under submission to the truth of God's Word, but eventually such feelings and thoughts will be conquered. We will be released from the bondage of distortion, and we will gradually conform to the Word of God.

Feelings can be trusted only when they are ruled by the Lord as we harmonize our thinking with His truth. If our emotions are not in submission to the Lord, we are operating in the flesh. When the Bible speaks of "the flesh," it is often referring to a cooperation of the body and the soul in which the bodily appetites or the emotions call the shots. In such a position, the will is weak. On the other hand, when we choose to believe and obey the Word of God, our will gets stronger, so that we are no longer ruled by passion and lust, "indulging the desires of the flesh and of the mind" (Ephesians 2:3).

Another thought pattern that can become a putrid prison is that of blame. Blame is like a merry-go-round that goes around and around until everyone gets dizzy and sick. At first the ride may be enjoyable because we let ourselves off the hook. However, as the blaming goes on, we get the blame as well as give it. There seems to be no end and no answer. Blame began in the Garden of

Eden. Adam blamed both Eve and God (who had given Eve to him). Eve blamed the serpent. No one said, "I sinned against God and take full responsibility for my own sin." Taking personal responsibility for personal sin, rather than casting blame, is the first exit off the merry-go-round.

The second mental exit from the merry-go-round of blame is choosing to deal with problems by looking for solutions rather than casting blame. Although there are times when fault must be established, blaming is not necessary in problem-solving. When we travel, Martin drives and I read the maps and give directions. I have really goofed at times, but I am very grateful that he doesn't cast blame when I make mistakes. One time I thought we could take a shortcut to avoid heavy freeway traffic in an unfamiliar area. My "shortcut" took us about two hours out of our way. Although we had to contend with being lost and late, our relationship did not suffer. Because of Martin's choice not to cast blame, our relationship became even stronger.

Besides preventing logical problem-solving, blaming can ruin relationships and feed unforgiveness, bitterness, and hatred. For some people, blaming is a habit. As soon as something goes wrong, they cast blame at someone. The problem is then intensified by the soured relationship. Blaming others seeks to justify self, fosters pride, stimulates self-pity, and ultimately backfires into self-condemnation, because if there's no one else to blame we blame ourselves. One of the surest ways out of self-condemnation, next to believing God's Word, is to choose not to cast blame.

Our thinking is so important that it is the first line of defense against the enemy It is also the devil's primary battleground. That is why Paul wrote:

> Though we walk in the flesh, we do not war according to the flesh, for the weapons of our warfare are not of the flesh, but divinely powerful for the destruction of fortresses. We are destroying speculations and every lofty thing raised up against the knowledge of God, and we are taking every thought captive to the obedience of Christ (2 Corinthians 10:3-5).

The most violent battles are waged in the mind. It was through Eves *thinking* that Satan was able to entice her. Because he succeeded in diminishing her faith, hope, and love, he was able to get her to eat the fruit. Eve fell because she did not check every thought with God. She could have cast down the devil's vain speculations by submitting the ideas to God, but instead she allowed thoughts of selfish desire to take precedence over thoughts of God and His word of warning.

Temptation is always the same: It begins in the mind. It may be only a flash of an idea quickly followed, but it is there in the mind first. Even if it is not a clear idea, it is there nevertheless as an attitude, a frame of mind, or a desire. However, by submitting every thought to the scrutiny of Christ, we can cast down speculations and vain imagination. We can bring "every thought captive to the obedience of Christ."

The ballet dancer submits her thoughts to the obedience of the instruction. As a combination of movements is given, she learns the combination instead of making one up on her own. Her mind is active as she attempts to learn and remember the sequence of steps. Her mind and body work together as she moves from one step to the next. She must also remember the details of directions she has been given in order to perform each step correctly. Just a simple combination of six movements requires the dancer to bring every thought into submission to the instructor. If the dancer's mind wanders, she will be embarrassed when she alone fails to do the combination as directed.

The ballet dancer not only fills her mind with the details of instruction and with each new sequence of movements; she must also use her mind creatively as she seeks to express the mind of the one who has choreographed the sequence of movements. Likewise, as we fill our minds with details from the Word of God and follow the guidance of the Holy Spirit throughout the day, we too enter into the creativity of the Lord as He works in us and through us. As well as filling our minds with God and His Word, we are to think according to truth and righteousness.

> Finally, brethren, whatever is true, whatever is honorable, whatever is right, whatever is pure, whatever is lovely whatever is of good repute, if there is any excellence and if anything worthy of praise, let your mind dwell on these things. The things you have learned and received and heard and seen in me, practice these things; and the God of peace shall be with you (Philippians 4:8, 9).

Devotional Exercise

1. Read Psalm 138 several times. Think about it and write down how the words of the psalmist apply to you. Is there something in the psalm that encourages you to do something new or different?

2. Read Isaiah 26:3, 4. Are you trapped in any habit of thinking, such as fear, blame, bitterness, or unbelief? What does God want you to do about it?

3. Read Philippians 4:8, 9. Notice throughout the day what kinds of things go into your mind. Which things match Philippians 4:8? Which do not? What might you do about improving your mental diet?

11

More Discipline:
The Tongue

I could not believe that I was actually there. Excitement coursed through every part of me as I stood before the originals! I was familiar with prints of Monet, Degas, Manet, and Van Gogh, but the power of the original paintings—one right next to the other—overwhelmed me. I felt a profound respect for the artists who conceived and communicated such beauty and passion. The intense drama of life and the quiet moments of solitude had been spoken with a brush dipped in paint.

The paintings displayed in the Museum of Impressionism at the Louvre surprised me beyond expectation. We had been respectfully and almost reverently viewing works of the great masters throughout Europe. Yet this concentration of Impressionism was the high point for me. Degas had been a favorite of mine for years because he had respect for the dance. He understood and communicated the delicate balance between technique and art, between the precision of the class and the ethereal nature of the performance.

Respect for art comes only from knowing that the artist is not only gifted but has devoted much of his life to perfecting his art. It's not just a fly-by-night craft that he just picked up, but rather a combination of skill, perception, and a great deal of study and work. Some dabblers have little respect for great art; they may have done a little painting and been satisfied. Some dabblers in theater have no true respect for acting even though they once acted in a play. Some dilettantes have no appreciation for the dedication and years of hard work that it takes to make a truly great actor. Likewise, some dabblers in Christianity have no respect for the intensity of devotion to which the Lord has called His children. They have perhaps read a bit of the Bible and think they know the ins and outs of walking with God.

A very wise ballet teacher told me the story of a woman who bounced into his studio one day and announced that she needed to learn ballet in two weeks. She insisted that she could learn quickly, and she confessed that she had already accepted a job to teach ballet in another city. The teacher took a deep breath. How preposterous! He tried to explain the impossibility of such a task. But when she announced that she would get the training somewhere else if he wouldn't do it, he decided to do what he could to prevent her from harming her future students. For two solid weeks he taught her the elementary principles of the five ballet positions, the *plié*, the *tendu*, and the *degagé*. The woman learned at least one thing during the two weeks—the difficulty of controlling every part of her body while performing even the most basic movements in ballet. The teacher never heard what happened to the woman, but I think she must have developed some respect for ballet.

In treating any art form with respect, we not only appreciate the skill that is required but we keep things in proper perspective. We do not expect a beginner to succeed rapidly. Yet, in the Christian walk we seem to expect believers to change rapidly. We forget that God gives many of us years and years to learn how to think, speak, and act according to His design. We must have respect for the Christian walk and patience with one another.

One part of me will take a lifetime to master, even though I use the instrument every day. I have not yet mastered my tongue even as much as I had once mastered other parts of my body for ballet. However, I have learned that I cannot afford to be a dabbler, careless in what I say, because the tongue is a powerful instrument. It more resembles a burning torch than a brush of paint. King David prayed:

> Let the words of my mouth and the meditation of my heart
>
> Be acceptable in Thy sight,
>
> O Lord, my rock and my Redeemer (Psalm 19:14).

The tongue is more difficult to control than any other part of the body, even though it is usually easier to say a kind word than to perform a dazzling gymnastic feat. Even the most intricate movement in ballet takes less control than that which the tongue regularly requires. An artist who knows God and understands the nature of the tongue will surely agree that he can control the paint and the brush more easily than he can control his own tongue. James graphically described how difficult it is to keep the tongue under control.

> We all stumble in many ways. If anyone does not stumble in what he says, he is a perfect man, able to bridle the whole body as well. Now if we put the bits into the horses' mouths so that they may obey us, we direct their entire body as well. Behold, the ships also, though they are so great and are driven by strong winds, are still directed by a very small rudder, wherever the inclination of the pilot desires.
>
> So also the tongue is a small part of the body and yet it boasts of great things. Behold, how great a forest is set aflame by such a small fire! And the tongue is a fire, the very world of iniquity; the tongue is set among our members as that which defiles the entire body, and sets on fire the course of our life, and is set on fire by hell.
>
> For every species of beasts and birds, of reptiles and creatures of the sea, is tamed and has been tamed by the human race. But no one can tame the tongue; it is a restless evil and full of deadly poison. With it we bless our Lord and Father, and with it we curse men, who have been made in the likeness of God; from the same mouth come both blessing and cursing. My brethren, these things ought not to be this way (James 3:2-10).

Sounds impossible, doesn't it? And yet our Lord is the God of the impossible. He will enable us to control our tongue as we put ourselves under His control.

There is a kind of hierarchy of order that works with the tongue. Although it is a powerful instrument for good and for evil, and although it can operate like the rudder on a ship, we must remember that the pilot is greater than the rudder. The pilot is the one who turns the rudder. God has given us the position of pilot over our own tongue. By our choices we turn the tongue to good or to evil. By choice we speak a word of truth or a lie. By choice we speak a word to edify or to destroy. By choice we speak love or hate. It all depends on the condition of the pilot.

For the Christian woman to exercise proper control over her tongue, she must have her life in the order that God has designed. When Jesus came to live in her, He came to set things right. He came to take authority as Lord. As long as she respects His authority, places her will under submission to Him, and thinks according to righteousness, truth, and love, her words will come forth from that relationship of love. However, if she slips and allows her own cleverness, her own emotions, and her own bodily appetites to supersede the authority of her Lord for even a moment, she will not have godly control of her tongue.

Proverbs reminds us of the relationship of the heart to the tongue. Our inner attitudes, motivations, thoughts, and emotions will affect our speaking even if we succeed in hiding them for a season.

> He who walks in integrity walks securely, but he who perverts his ways will be found out. He who

winks the eye causes trouble, and a babbling fool will be thrown down. The mouth of the righteous is a fountain of life, but the mouth of the wicked conceals violence.... On the lips of the discerning, wisdom is found (Proverbs 10:9-11, 13).

He who conceals hatred has lying lips, and he who spreads slander is a fool. When there are many words, transgression is unavoidable, but he who restrains his lips is wise. The tongue of the righteous is as choice silver; The heart of the wicked is worth little. The lips of the righteous feed many (Proverbs 10:18-21).

What a contrast! The tongue can be used for life or violence, wisdom or foolishness, good or evil, nourishment or destruction. It all depends on what is going on behind the tongue.

In his letter to the Ephesians, Paul preceded his directions for godly speech with an admonition to put off the former manner of life and to "be renewed in the spirit of your mind, and put on the new self, which in the likeness of God has been created in righteousness and holiness of the truth" (Ephesians 4:22-24). He reminds us of our relationship with God in new life before he gives important directions concerning the tongue. He then gives three essential replacements: truth rather than falsehood, wholesomeness rather than harmfulness, and kindness rather than wrath and malice.

Truthful

As we read Paul's admonition to speak only the truth, we say "Amen." After all, we are honest folks, or so we think.

> Laying aside falsehood, speak truth, each one of you, with his neighbor, for we are members of one another (Ephesians 4:25).

We readily agree that speaking the truth is the Christian way to talk.

> Put away from you a deceitful mouth, and put devious lips far from you (Proverbs 4:24).

Deceptive speech, however, includes more than out-and-out lies. It includes the half-truths of telling only what we want a listener to hear. As it is, we are limited to our own perspective in observing any event, let alone those in which we are emotionally involved. Other forms of deception come with exaggeration. Some exaggeration is used merely as a figure of speech (hyperbole) to emphasize a point. However, it is deception when expressed as fact. Many Christians are guilty of what some of us label "evangelical exaggeration."

One of the most destructive forms of lying that Christians engage in is that of gossip and rumor. Rather than checking out the facts, they take what others say and spread it around. Terrible rumors, which have no foundation in fact, have ruined the reputations of fellow Christians.

Even more dangerous is the deception perpetrated in certain faith-healing events. Recent investigative reporting has exposed certain faith healers who were actually using devices of their own cunning, while claiming supernatural knowledge and pronouncing healings. Many of the deceived people discontinued medical treatment for diseases which had not been healed at all. Such dishonesty not only leads Christians astray; it turns unsaved people away from Christianity altogether.

For our words to be accurate, we have to be careful to check everything with the facts. We want to believe God in faith, but we do not want to be gullible to half-truths, as glorious as they may sound. God always deals with truth; there is no deception in Him or in His Word. To reflect His character we also want to speak only that which is true, honest, and just.

Wholesome

Besides measuring our words against the standard of truth and honesty, we need to evaluate whether or not the words we choose to say will build up another person in faith hope, and love or tear him down. Paul put it this way:

> Let no unwholesome word proceed from your mouth, but only such a word as is good for edification according to the need of the moment, that it may give grace to those who hear (Ephesians 4:29).

Unwholesome words tear down rather than build up people in faith, hope, and love. This means more than just saying nice things to people. A wholesome word may be a word of exhortation or encouragement, just as Paul wrote:

> But speaking the truth in love, we are to grow
> up in all aspects into Him who is the head, even
> Christ (Ephesians 4:15).

The motivation is always to build the person up, not to tear him down. And the manner of speaking is always "in love." The purpose of everything we say to another person should be "good for edification according to the need of the moment, that it may give grace to those who hear."

We may think that ordering our speech to edify and give grace to the listener would apply only when we are "ministering" to another person or "witnessing." No, this is for all speech. It applies while giving instructions to a worker, while ordering from a menu at the restaurant, while disciplining the children, while trying to get a point across to someone with a different point of view. There is more involved than the words themselves; the emotional components of expression sometimes speak far louder than the words themselves. The volume also communicates grace or unwholesomeness. There is no formula for this; neither can we plan much of what we say in advance. Rather, the speech must come from the throne of grace on which our Lord sits as Ruler of our hearts. If every thought is brought into captivity to Jesus, every word will also be under submission to Him. We must walk closely with our Lord in order to speak edification and grace to those around us.

Controlling the tongue is difficult for those of us who talk a lot. I am a talker, and I think out loud much of the time. Therefore I am at greater risk of disobeying the Lord with my mouth than the person who says little. This does not mean that I need to stop talking, but that I must refrain from unwholesome speech. I need to speak according to God's wisdom and love so that my words will indeed minister grace.

The importance of our speech cannot be minimized. I have heard words of cruelty escape from people's lips in snide, under-handed remarks, as though the speaker has no comprehension of the seriousness of what he is doing. I have heard husbands make unkind remarks about their wives in the guise of joking with the guys. I have heard women talk about their husbands in ways that tear down their own households. Rather than building their house with wisdom, they are inheriting the wind.

> He who troubles his own house Will inherit the wind (Proverbs 11:29).

> By wisdom a house is built, and by understanding it is established; and by knowledge the rooms are filled with all precious and pleasant riches (Proverbs 24:3,4).

Unwholesome speech and careless words are grievous to the Lord. Right after the admonition to speak only those things which will give grace to the listener, the Holy Spirit inspired Paul to write:

> Do not grieve the Holy Spirit of God, by whom you were sealed for the day of redemption (Ephesians 4:30).

Have we ever realized how often we must grieve the Holy Spirit with our careless words? Jesus spoke about the seriousness of our speech:

> I say to you that every careless word that men
> shall speak, they shall render account for it in the
> day of judgment. For by your words you shall
> be justified, and by your words you shall be
> condemned (Matthew 12:36, 37).

These sound like harsh words, but they were true and
necessary for the moment. If these words strike us and
we know that we are guilty of careless words, we have an
Advocate with the Father. Rather than condemnation, we
can receive forgiveness based upon the blood of Jesus
Christ. Every careless or cruel word that passes our lips
is a signal that we have slipped in our walk with Jesus.
We need to turn back to Him and confess that we have
sinned. When we confess, He forgives us and we are
reestablished in close fellowship with Him, so that we
may walk in righteousness and speak what is wholesome
and good (1 John 1:9).

Kind

Besides speaking only what is true and what edifies
and ministers grace to the listener, we are to measure all
that we say by the standard of kindness.

> Let all bitterness and wrath and anger and clamor
> and slander be put away from you, along with all
> malice. And be kind to one another, tenderhearted,
> forgiving each other, just as God in Christ also
> has forgiven you (Ephesians 4:31, 32).

Just as a ballet dancer checks herself moment by
moment with the help of a mirror, we need to look at
what we say and take responsibility for it. We could use
both lists included in these verses to check our speech.

The list includes those things which need to be put away. Words of bitterness, wrath, anger, clamor, slander, and malice will not come from a right relationship with the Father. On the other hand, words of kindness come from a right relationship with the Father, one in which the heart is tender and ready to forgive. We need to be like the godly woman in Proverbs:

> She opens her mouth in wisdom, and the teaching of kindness is on her tongue (Proverbs 31:26).

I have respect for all the time and effort that go into a work of art and into the training of an actor or a dancer. But even more, I have deep respect for those who have brought the tongue under the control of the blessed Holy Spirit. A tongue which expresses truth in love, which edifies and gives grace in wisdom, and which follows the law of kindness is a treasure worth more than all the paintings in the world.

> Like apples of gold in settings of silver
> Is a word spoken in right circumstances.
> Like an earring of gold and an ornament of fine gold
> Is a wise reprover to a listening ear (Proverbs 25:11,12).

Let us with patience develop a tongue which paints truth and a mouth which speaks wisdom in grace.

Devotional Exercise

In each of these exercises you will be using the mirror of the Word of God.

1. Read and meditate on Ephesians 4:25 and Proverbs 10:9-13, 18-21. Use these verses throughout several days as a mirror by which to evaluate your speech. If you fail to have a perfect score, use 1 John 1:9.

2. Read and meditate on Ephesians 4:29; Proverbs 11:29 and 24:3, 4; and Matthew 12:36, 37. Use these verses for several days after you have completed the above assignment. Again use the Word of God as a mirror to evaluate your speech. Remember also to use 1 John 1:9 whenever necessary.

3. This time use Ephesians 4:30-32; Psalm 19:14; and Proverbs 31:26 as your mirror. Once again 1 John 1:9 may be necessary.

12

The Choreographer: Submission to Him

A ballet is not simply a dance, but rather a drama in movement or an expression of ideas and moods. The choreographer is the person who creates a ballet just as a playwright writes a play. The ballet may be a fanciful story or a series of imagined interplays of color, design, and movement. The ballet may also reveal a glimpse of truth which the choreographer has perceived. The choreographer creates the theme, drama, and mood of the ballet by combining movement and music. He chooses the musical score and arranges the dancers and steps to portray his story and/or theme. He also chooses dancers who can best dance the roles in the way he envisions them. He must know each dancer's capabilities and weaknesses so that he can build on their strengths for optimum performance. With artistic sensibility, down-to-earth reality, and calculating judgment, he creates the dance.

God is more than a choreographer, because His creation includes the entire universe. Whereas a choreographer creates something out of what is available, God created out of nothing. He spoke and the world came into being. And yet, He has not simply created us and gone His way. No. He involves Himself with His creation in such a way as to guide and sustain us, to provide the means of relationship, and to recreate us into the image of Christ.

God is both our creator and our re-creator. Jesus is the "author and finisher of our faith. Besides being our creator, He creates our walk in Him. He leads us in paths of righteousness for His name's sake. He orders our steps. God is a trustworthy choreographer. He knows us so well that He knows what we can do and what we cannot do.

Because a ballet dancer performs what the choreographer has created, she must place herself in submission to him. She must seek to know what he is attempting to convey through each sequence of movements. But she is not simply a puppet performing like a robot: She has a soul; she has ideas and emotions; she has her own manner of expression. She has a great deal to add to the role.

The choreographer works with the dancer to enable her to convey his intent. To obtain the best performance, he will give her a role that fits her ability and even her personality. Certain parts require the sensitivity and maturity that a young dancer may lack. Certain dancers are best at stunning parts that require great technical skill. Others excel in slow adagio or romantic parts. There is something that goes beyond training that a choreographer desires to enhance. It is this "something" that makes the difference between a sensitive artist and simply a skilled dancer. Some dancers can make a part live while others simply perform the steps well.

The artistic sensibility of the dancer is her greatest asset. The choreographer will attempt to make the most of that special quality while creating the steps which make up the whole dance. The greatest choreographers treat the dancers as fellow artists, not simply as tools or instruments. At the same time, the dancer who excels in conveying the choreographer's intent is the one who learns what he wants and submits to his leadership.

The very word *submission* makes some of us wince, and yet submission is an absolute necessity in working with a choreographer. Submission is not simply mindless subservience, as some may think. Nor does submission make us inferior. Neither is submission a type of submersion into nothingness. Submission is more than obedience, because it is a heart attitude of cooperation. It is not simply doing what another person says outwardly while inwardly disagreeing. Submission can never be forced. Although force may be exerted on someone and that person may comply, true submission is voluntary.

I must confess that I have not always been submissive in working with choreographers. While dancing with an opera company, I objected to a certain series of steps. They were awkward and did not seem to go with the music or the role. I expressed my concern to the choreographer. She did not agree with me and wanted me to do the steps as directed. I did as she directed, but I was not submissive. Every time I came to that sequence of steps I exaggerated them to make them look ridiculous and out of place. She did change the steps, but only because she figured I couldn't do them as she had intended. Although

I got my way, I used devious means and was far from submissive. If I had continued in this vein I would eventually have been replaced by another dancer.

The Lord calls us into willing submission to Him. He does not want to force us, neither is He oppressive in His dealings with us. He desires to bring out His best through us. Yet, for us to be fully submissive to Him, we must trust Him. Just as a choreographer may work through an artistic director or a rehearsal director, the Lord puts us under human leadership as well. Thus our submission to the Lord will be expressed through willing cooperation and submission to those He puts over us in leadership, whether in the church, the home, or the workplace. Whenever we are in rebellion to the leadership He has provided, we have to check to see if we are in submission to the Lord.

Our Great Choreographer knows us. But do we know Him? Do we know Him enough to trust Him directly? Do we know Him enough to trust Him when we are under the leadership of a person who is not as kind and wise as He is? An accurate view of God is essential for an intimate walk of trust and submission. Yet few of us have 20-20 vision in perceiving the majesty and righteousness of God as well as His love and compassion. Jesus came to clear our vision. First He revealed God in the flesh as He walked among us nearly 2000 years ago. Then He died in our place for our sin, which had clouded and distorted our spiritual perception. And then He sent His Holy Spirit to open our spiritual eyes.

A great deal of human suffering has resulted from a misunderstanding of the character of God. Some see Him as an exacting taskmaster who reaps where he does not sow. Others see Him as vindictive and punitive. Some see Him as an omnipotent force with no personal involvement with people. Others see Him as an indulgent Santa Claus. Still others see Him as a God of unconditional love and acceptance who simply overlooks our wrong-doing.

The character of God is impossible to understand through mere human knowledge, because He is spiritual. He does not have the same distorted emotions and motivations that we have, neither is He limited in any kind of knowledge. He is not like us, though we were created to be like Him. We cannot truly know God by looking at ourselves or even by looking at each other. However, we may discover who we are by looking at God. Furthermore, by focusing accurately and consistently on the glory of the Lord (which includes His character), believers are transformed into His likeness:

> We all, with unveiled face beholding as in a mirror the glory of the Lord, are being transformed into the same image from glory to glory just as from the Lord, the Spirit (2 Corinthians 3:18).

Paul's highest ambition in life was to know God intensely and intimately: "that I may know Him, and the power of His resurrection and the fellowship of His sufferings, being conformed to His death (Philippians 3:10).

Many religions of the world would reduce God to an impersonal force or as one great mind of which we are all a part. However, the God revealed in the Bible is a Person. He is not an impersonal force or power. Furthermore, He is transcendent, far greater than His creation. Though He may fill all the earth, the earth is not an extension of Him. He is not merged with His creation, though creation is dependent on Him.

The most fundamental facet of God's character is love. God's love under girds, amplifies, and modifies every aspect of His being. His love is expressed in His power, in His truth, and in His grace. Within these three categories of God's love are a multitude of descriptions and numerous examples throughout Scripture. However, it is important to keep these three areas in mind, because distortion often comes from considering God's attributes within one category without including the balance of the other categories. For example, to see God as all-powerful without mercy and goodness would be extremely frightening. Yet, this is exactly how some people view God, and they suffer for it. To see God with only the mercy side of His love, without justice and truth, would reduce Him to a doting parent who simply spoils his child and does not care if he does what is right.

Individuals differ in their view of God just as the blind men perceived the elephant. Depending on the part of the elephant he felt, each one ventured his opinion: a tree, a wall, a rope, a spear, a snake. Then in great confidence each began to argue and defend his position. The woman of God, on the other hand, desires to perfect her vision of God by looking at Him through His Word, through prayer, and through obedience.

God's Power

Perhaps the most obviously majestic and awesome of the attributes of God lie within the first category: God as source and creator of all life, matter, and energy. His might and power are expressed in the name *Elohim*, which means "mighty God." His existence as the source of life, apart from any other source or power, is expressed in the name He revealed to Moses: *Jehovah*, which means "I am that I am." The God of the Bible is the very source of life. Because Jesus is in the divine Trinity, He is also the life source.

> In the beginning was the Word, and the Word was with God, and the Word was God. He was in the beginning with God. All things came into being by Him, and apart from Him nothing came into being that has come into being. In Him was life, and the life was the light of men (John 1:1-4).

In speaking of Christ, Paul said:

> He is the image of the invisible God, the first-born of all creation. For by Him all things were created both in the heavens and on earth, visible and invisible, whether thrones or dominions or rulers or authorities—all things have been created by Him and for Him. And He is before all things, and in Him all things hold together (Colossians 1:15-17).

It is important to know that God is able to give life and that He is powerful and all-knowing. Without this understanding a woman could feel very helpless within her circumstances.

When a woman comprehends something of the power of God and when she realizes that God extends His power on her behalf, she is more likely to have the courage to trust and obey Him. Paul therefore prayed that "the eyes of your heart may be enlightened, so that you may know...what is the surpassing greatness of His power toward us who believe" (Ephesians 1:18, 19). Just considering the strength of God may give a woman the amount of strength necessary to go through a difficult time.

> There is none like the God of Jeshurun [Israel], Who rides the heavens to your help, and through the skies in His majesty. The eternal God is a dwelling place, and underneath are the everlasting arms.... (Deuteronomy 33:26, 27).

God is the sovereign ruler who will set right the injustices and the wrongs of society which oppress men and women. When everything seems to be going wrong, a woman may take confidence in the fact that God is there. He is the Lord of the moment as well as of eternity. A woman needs to keep these truths in her heart and mind because they provide God's dimension to each situation. When a woman knows that God truly controls all things, she can handle one aspect of a problem without being overwhelmed by the entire situation.

Within God's almighty ability is the fact of His omniscience and His constant presence. God is present everywhere, and nothing escapes His awareness. Job proclaimed, "His eyes are upon the ways of a man, and He sees all his steps" (Job 34:21). Job found strength to persevere in the fact that God knows. When people misunderstand us, God knows.

When a woman knows the character of God, there is great comfort in the fact that God knows everything about her. However, without an accurate view of God, the fact that God knows could engender fear. Just after

Adam sinned, his vision of God was distorted and he hid from the presence of God. Nevertheless, when we know God's love and care for us, we can be encouraged by His all-knowing and ever-present capabilities. Then we can find comfort and strength from Psalm 139.

> O Lord, Thou hast searched me and known me. Thou dost know when I sit down and when I rise up; Thou dost understand my thought from afar. Thou dost scrutinize my path and my lying down, and art intimately acquainted with all my ways. Even before there is a word on my tongue, Behold, 0 Lord, Thou dost know it all. Thou hast enclosed me behind and before, and laid Thy hand upon me. Such knowledge is too wonderful for me; it is too high, I cannot attain to it (Psalm 139:1-6).

The Word of God is full of reminders of God's supernatural abilities and His personal concern. Jesus reminds us, "With men this is impossible, but with God all things are possible" (Matthew 19:26). Psalm 147:5 declares, "Great is our Lord, and abundant in strength; His understanding is infinite." Moses' final words to Israel included these words:

> Be strong and courageous; do not be afraid or tremble at them, for the Lord your God is the one who goes with you. He will not fail you or forsake you (Deuteronomy 31:6).

God's Truth

The second category of the character of God centers in truth and involves the very holiness of God. He is righteous and just. He is wise and trustworthy. God has limited Himself to speaking only truth and to keeping every one of His promises. He can be fully counted on, for He is consistent in all His ways. Individuals who have grown up with lies, broken promises, and unreliable people may have a difficult time believing that anyone, even God, can be honest, true, and dependable. They need to see these attributes of God through reading the Bible and through a growing experience of learning to trust Him.

Too often both men and women trust their own thoughts and feelings more than they trust God. If the ideas and feelings differ from what God has said, a choice must be made. If God's Word is true and the feelings say something different, the feelings must be unreliable indicators of the truth. For example, God has said that He would never leave us or forsake us. Do we always sense the presence of God? We may feel utterly alone. Which is true—God's Word or my faulty perception? If God says that He loves us, who are we to deny that He does? A great deal of misery and confusion comes from not believing what God has said. Unless we trust God, we can easily slip into fear, self-centered concern, and anxiety.

God does not change His ways, neither is He one to alter His Word. Balaam discovered this fact when he attempted to curse Israel after God had said that Israel was blessed:

> God is not a man, that He should lie, nor a son
> of man, that He should repent; has he said, and
> will he not do it? or has He spoken, and will
> He not make it good? Behold, I have received a
> command to bless; when He has blessed, then I
> cannot revoke it (Numbers 23:19, 20).

The consistency of God exists throughout the Trinity: "Jesus Christ is the same yesterday and today, yes and forever" (Hebrews 13:8). Even if people change and fail, God never does. Feelings change; God does not. He can be completely trusted. Since He is trustworthy we can confidently place our trust in Him. As we know and trust Him, we will love and obey Him. God's wisdom is also based upon truth. Though the enemy may be crafty and sly, he is not wise because he is deceptive.

God's wisdom never strays from truth. His wisdom is so far above our wisdom that Paul said, "The foolishness of God is wiser than men" (1 Corinthians 1:25). His wisdom surpasses our intellect and imagination. We may sometimes misunderstand God's actions because we do not comprehend His wisdom. For example, if God has the power to change an individual's circumstances and if He indeed loves that person, why does He not always intervene? His wisdom and knowledge often prevent Him from exercising His power in a given situation.

God's truth also includes His justice. Even though the circumstances of life may not be fair, God is just. People who do not know God often blame Him for the evil in the world. They do not understand that evil is the result of the sins of mankind and the craftiness of Satan. Whenever a person persists in hanging onto his own distorted concept of God, he is actually placing his own opinion above the Word of God. Such persistence may indeed occur in one's concept of justice if that person has become his own standard for what is fair and for what is right and wrong. When a person does not regard God as fair, he sets himself up as a judge of God and will remain in corruption until he chooses to believe and trust God.

Furthermore, there may be some confusion between justice and mercy Justice says, "All have sinned, and fall short of the glory of God," and, "The wages of sin is death" (Romans 3:23 and 6:23). If there are two criminals who have been tried for their crimes and correctly condemned, justice and fairness have been accomplished. However, if the governor extends a pardon, that is an act of grace and mercy. Many people would then say that it is unfair of the governor to extend mercy to one person and not to the other, but mercy is beyond justice. Justice and fairness do not provide salvation, because we all deserve condemnation. Salvation is all grace and mercy. When God's grace and mercy are given beyond justice, anyone who judges God as unfair is incorrect in his judgment. Grace and mercy cannot be judged by fairness and justice guidelines. "For the wages of sin is death, but the free gift of God is eternal life in Christ Jesus our Lord" (Romans 6:23). God is completely fair and just, but His justice is graced with love and mercy, which do not in any way diminish His justice.

Holiness is another attribute of God which is connected to truth. God's holiness is such that He is absolute perfection without a single blemish. His character is pure and good without a flaw. Nothing He does is wrong. He has limited His great power with His character of holiness. With great power and might one could destroy and perform great evil, as indeed Satan and his followers attempt to do. The God of the Bible, however, will not use His power to do anything that would contradict His holiness and righteousness.

Since God is morally perfect and it is impossible for Him to do wrong, He is the standard for what is right. "Righteous art Thou, O Lord, and upright are Thy judgments" (Psalm 119:137). When God's ways differ from our own, we tend to rebel. God's standards of righteousness and holiness reveal our own shortcomings. That is why some people avoid the idea of a perfect and righteous God. And yet, when we are looking for truth and a standard of righteousness higher than ourselves, we are surely relieved to discover a righteous and holy God.

> The Lord is righteous in all His ways, and kind in all His deeds. The Lord is near to all who call upon Him, to all who call upon Him in truth. He will fulfill the desire of those who fear Him; He will also hear their cry and will save them. The Lord keeps all who love Him; but all the wicked He will destroy. My mouth will speak the praise of the Lord; and all flesh will bless His holy name forever and ever (Psalm 145:17-21).

The holiness of God, however, does pose a problem for sinful humanity for without the love of God the holiness separates humans from God. How can a sinful person dare approach the holiness of God? The great chasm between the sinfulness of mankind and the holiness of God put fear in the Israelites as they approached Mount Sinai. The holiness of God forbade them to come near.

Sinners cannot approach a holy God on the basis of personal merit, for the Scripture says that "all our righteous deeds are like a filthy garment" (Isaiah 64:6). The apostle Paul emphasized this fact when he quoted from the Psalms:

> There is none righteous, not even one; There is none who understands, There is none who seeks for God; All have turned aside, together they have become useless; There is none who does good. There is not even one (Romans 3:10-12).

The only way a sinful person can enter into the presence of a holy God is to have all sin removed, to be cleansed, and to be made holy.

God's Grace

The love of God is such a prominent feature of His character that the apostle John wrote, "God is love" (1 John 4:8). God created us for relationship with Himself. He loved us before the foundation of the world, even before He made Adam and Eve. He loved Adam and Eve before they sinned and He loved them after they sinned. His love has continued throughout all time and reaches out to every individual.

However, the combination of His love with His holiness posed a dilemma which only God could solve: the dilemma of a holy God loving an unholy people when there can be no fellowship of light with darkness. God's solution to His great love for us was the cross of Christ.

> God so loved the world that He gave His only begotten Son, that whoever believes in Him

should not perish, but have eternal life (John 3:16).

This God chose to do in spite of the great price required: the death of Jesus on the cross. Jesus chose to make that supreme sacrifice because of love. In Jesus grace and truth were joined together in such a way as to maintain truth and justice while ministering grace. That is why the apostle John declared:

> Of His fulness we have all received, and grace upon grace. For the Law was given through Moses; grace and truth were realized through Jesus Christ (John 1:16, 17).

Only through the death and resurrection of Jesus could God extend His love and mercy and grace to mankind. Jesus is the only way to the Father. He said, "I am the way, and the truth, and the life; no one comes to the Father but through Me" (John 14:6). Only through receiving God's love, forgiveness, and grace on the basis of the cross can men and women approach a holy God.

Many people who suffer from a distorted concept of God cannot experience His love, because they attempt to earn His love. They look within themselves and decide whether or not they deserve His love. They do not realize that they are loved because of God's grace, not because of their own merit. No woman can understand the love of God by looking at herself, because no one loves the way God loves. His love is not contaminated by sin or any kind of selfish motivation. God's love is so tremendously giving that He was willing to pay the full price for the sins of mankind in order to be able to extend and express that love to you and to me.

While we were still helpless, at the right time Christ died for the ungodly. For one will hardly die for a righteous man, though perhaps for the good man someone would dare even to die. But God demonstrates His own love toward us in that, while we were yet sinners, Christ died for us (Romans 5:6-8).

Paul rejoiced that although we "were by nature children of wrath . . . God, being rich in mercy, because of His great love with which He loved us, even when we were dead in our transgressions, made us alive together with Christ (by grace you have been saved)" (Ephesians 2:3-5).

Jesus lived a completely obedient life, without flaw and without sin. In doing so He fulfilled the holy law of God, which was unattainable by sinful human beings. If anyone could fulfill the whole law, including the Ten Commandments, the ordinances of the Law of Moses, and the Sermon on the Mount, then perhaps there would be a way into the holy presence of God. However no one could do this until Jesus was born of the virgin. When He fulfilled the law He did not do it for Himself, but rather for the sake of fallen humanity. Jesus is the only Person who used His free will completely to obey God the Father and to live in perfect relationship to Him.

Jesus was "tempted in all things as we are, yet without sin" Hebrews 4:15). Even at the point of rejection by men and of looking at the sin He would have to bear on their behalf, Jesus purposed to do His Father's will in order to provide the means for a love relationship between God and us.

The person who does not understand the merciful and powerful significance of the cross will see it as an ineffectual waste, as a pitiful and cruel act of a wrathful God, or as a tragedy. However those who do know the purpose of Christ's sacrificial death and who appropriate all that the cross signifies become new creatures. Their old sinful self is counted null and void on the cross and Christ becomes to them "Christ in you, the hope of glory" (Colossians 1:27).

The cross of Christ is the great expression of the love of God and it is the key to the abundant life in Jesus. One way to realize the extent of Jesus' love is to proceed step-by-step through the pain and rejection which Jesus endured for you and for me. No matter what pain we may have experienced, Jesus experienced that pain on the cross. Every sin was upon Him; He fully identified with humanity both in His body and in His soul.

As you recall situations and people that have hurt you, fix your mind upon Jesus hanging on the cross. There He is, enduring the pain and saying, "Father, forgive them, for they do not know what they are doing" (Luke 23:34). He not only felt your pain but the pain that you have inflicted upon others. He offers forgiveness to you and He gives you the ability to forgive those who have harmed you. He knows the entire situation inside and out. Therefore He is able to restore you and He is able to restore them. He bore all this so that He could forgive, cleanse, and restore us. Jesus never said He would make life easy for us, but He did promise to be with us and to encompass us in His compassion and His healing forgiveness from the cross.

Although Jesus was never enslaved by fear, He identified with our fears on the cross. He knows the terror that grips many souls, and He came to set the captives free. Perhaps the greatest fears stem from the fear of death. Jesus, however, conquered death by way of the cross. Jesus "abolished death, and brought life and immortality to light through the gospel" (2 Timothy 1:10). Jesus knew that "through death He might render powerless him who had the power of death, that is, the devil; and might deliver those who through fear of death were subject to slavery all their lives" (Hebrews 2:14,15). We can bring each fear to the cross and give each one to Jesus. He understands and He is the remedy.

Jesus also suffered dire loneliness on the cross. When all of the ugliness of sin was upon Jesus, the sky hid its face in darkness. Jesus cried out, "My God, My God, why hast Thou forsaken Me?" (Mark 15:34). In the moments of His greatest pain, Jesus was encompassed in loneliness. He could not sense the strong, sweet presence of the Father whom He had always known. The heavy load of sin had become a thick wall of separation. He could not see the face of the Father until by faith He said, "Father, into Thy hands I commit My spirit" (Luke 23:46). The only way that this thick wall of separation between God and mankind could be broken was for Jesus to take upon Himself all of the sin and to suffer that separation Himself in the place of each sinner.

Jesus' death was necessary, for in cosmic legal terms justice had to be accomplished. Justice required payment for sin. Since justice alone, without mercy and grace, would send us all to eternal judgment, Jesus stepped into our place and took the punishment for every person who will believe and trust Him.

God's love flowed through the cross of Christ so that we could enter the relationship God had intended and so that God could enter our lives to give us the qualities of His own character: holiness, righteousness, justice, truth, faith, moral responsibility, love, forgiveness, and mercy. Although God maintains His own supremacy and power, He operates His kingdom and His power through the lives of His sons and daughters. An understanding of the character of God is just the beginning movement into knowing Him, experiencing His love and His life, becoming a vessel for His character, and growing into His likeness.

The Choreographer of our lives loves us and will direct us in paths of righteousness. He truly deserves our love and obedience, our faith and trust. If we follow His directions we will enter into His joy and walk in His ways. And while we also must bear a cross, it is only to crucify that within ourselves which He desires to change and fill with His character and His love. Our Choreographer's dance is a dance of love. He gives us the dance of transformation into the image of Christ.

Devotional Exercise

1. Read Psalm 89:1-37. List the attributes of God that you find in this psalm.

2. Write down verses that encourage you to trust God and submit to Him in every detail of your life.

3. Read Psalm 89:38-52. How important is it to submit to the Lord? What happened to the nation of Israel

when they no longer trusted God and rebelled? Why do you think the psalmist ends the psalm with praise?

13

Pas de Deux: The Discipline of Marriage

One of the most beautiful and exciting dances in a ballet is the *pas de deux*, which is a dance of relationship between a man and a woman. During the *pas de deux* both dancers work in such harmony that they become as one. At times they dance identical steps. At other times they dance corresponding steps, which enhance and complement the movements of the partner. There is such communion of movement that each responds to the other and each anticipates the movements of the other. The woman may run to the man and leap into his arms. He will catch her easily because he knows her timing and the manner of her leap.

The male dancer performs a great deal of supportive work in the *pas de deux*. He is there to hold the woman while she performs difficult extensions or multiple turns. He is there to guide her, to catch her, to lift her, to carry her. He not only dances his own part; he also enhances hers. She not only dances her part; she enhances his. Although mostly unspoken, the communication is constant between the two dancers in the *pas de deux*.

Our Great Choreographer created the first *pas de deux* in the Garden of Eden. After having brought all the animals to Adam there was found no created being that could fulfill the role of partner for him. Adam needed someone like himself to relate to as an equal being. He needed someone who was intelligent and who could thus willingly cooperate with him. He needed someone to share love on an equal plane of understanding, sympathy, and choice. He needed someone to correspond to himself.

God created Eve out of Adam's own flesh from a place near his heart. When Adam awoke and saw his bride, he immediately understood their oneness.

> The man said, "This is now bone of my bones and flesh of my flesh; She shall be called Woman, because she was taken out of Man." For this cause a man shall leave his father and his mother, and shall cleave to his wife; and they shall become one flesh (Genesis 2:23, 24).

God created the marriage relationship for love and for performing tasks that He assigned to mankind.

Although sin has marred the original design, the *pas de deux* continues for better or for worse. If the partners have believed on the Lord Jesus Christ and received new life, they are ready to follow the Great Choreographer's directions for the *pas de deux*. The Bible is full of instructions on cooperating with each other, submitting to God and also to each other, encouraging each other, and loving each other as God first loved us. Marriage is to be the basic human relationship within which children learn to live and to love.

Because each ballet dancer is human, there are flaws and shortcomings. The partners know each other's flaws more than anyone else. The male dancer will be very tuned into the weaknesses of the female and will attempt to compensate for them. If she habitually throws herself forward slightly during multiple turns, he will support her in such a way as to pull her back to center. If the man has a difficult time lifting the woman up onto his shoulder, she will jump harder to help him get her up there. There can be no competition, because the performance of one is dependent upon the performance of the other. One slip and there could be injury. Just as in ballet, marriage partners have to deal with each other's shortcomings. Thus both have ample opportunity to practice 1 Corinthians 13:

> Love is patient, love is kind, and is not jealous; love does not brag and is not arrogant, does not act unbecomingly; it does not seek its own, is not provoked, does not take into account a wrong suffered, does not rejoice in unrighteousness, but rejoices with the truth; bears all things, believes all things, hopes all things, endures all things. Love never fails (1 Corinthians 13:4-8).

What a beautiful description of the perfect *pas de deux* created by God!

In the *pas de deux* there is order of relationship. Both dancers perform many identical steps. However, when they dance as "one body" the male dancer does all the supportive work and the female dancer corresponds her movements to his. God has also designed order for the marriage relationship. Though marriage partners may attempt to manipulate the order to their own advantage, the biblical order is liberating if it is followed according to the law of the Spirit and the law of love. God used Paul to set forth the biblical order for the marriage relationship.

> I want you to understand that Christ is the head of every man, and the man is the head of a woman, and God is the head of Christ (1 Corinthians 11:3).

This order is essential. Only when the man is under the headship of Christ can he adequately serve his role of headship in marriage. If the woman herself is under the leadership of Christ as Lord in her life, she will place herself under the headship of her husband. Although it may be far easier to follow the leadership of a godly husband than that of a man who is not in submission to Christ, the woman will find that God is faithful to her if she follows His order in the relationship. Whenever the order breaks down, the relationship breaks down. If either dancer in the *pas de deux* moves out of the order of the choreographer or out of the traditional manner of performing the movements, the dance will fail to be what the choreographer intended.

In ballet the reason for the different responsibilities for each partner is obvious: the strength of the man and the grace of the woman. The reason for different roles for the man and woman in marriage may not be quite as clear. Both are intelligent. Both can make decisions.

Both have a degree of sensitivity. Both are equal, yet not the same. One could debate all sorts of reasons why the man is to be the leader in marriage, but the only valid, unchanging reason is that God has ordered it this way.

The order in marriage is part of God's remedy after the original disobedience in the Garden of Eden. Eve took the leadership when she gave Adam the forbidden fruit in the Garden. Adam followed her leadership and sinned. Whereas God had created both to reign together as partners under His authority and direction, God had to change the order of rulership because they were no longer in complete submission to Him.

> To the woman He said, "I will greatly multiply your pain in childbirth. In pain you shall bring forth children. Yet your desire shall be for your husband, and he shall rule over you."

> Then to Adam He said, "Because you have listened to the voice of your wife, and have eaten from the tree about which I commanded you, saying, 'You shall not eat from it'; cursed is the ground because of you; in toil you shall eat of it all the days of your life.... By the sweat of your face you shall eat bread, till you return to the ground, because from it you were taken; for you are dust, and to dust you shall return" (Genesis 3:16-19).

God's order in marriage is to promote righteousness, strength, honor, beauty, goodness, thoughtfulness, cooperation, unity of purpose, and love.

In their attempts to address certain social injustices against women, advocates of women's rights have often gone too far. Families have been destroyed. God's order has not only been abandoned, but ridiculed and trampled upon. Whereas worldly women complain that the Bible has taken away women's rights, the Bible has actually freed women from bondage and servitude. Before God's throne there is no difference between a slave and a freeman, between rich or poor, or between a man and a woman. The only difference comes through whether a person has called upon Jesus to be Savior and Lord. Although there is order, there is not preference. Both are of equal value in God's sight. Paul continues in 1 Corinthians:

> However, in the Lord, neither is woman independent of man nor is man independent of woman. For as the woman originates from the man, so also the man has his birth through the woman; and all things originate from God (1 Corinthians 11:11, 12).

Both the man and the woman are essential in the *pas de deux*. Neither partner can say that he or she is more important or less essential than the other.

God's designed order in marriage does not detract from the value of either partner. Rather, the order brings harmony and pictures the order of relationship between Christ and the church.

> Wives, be subject to your own husbands, as to the Lord. For the husband is the head of the wife, as Christ also is the head of the church, He Himself being the Savior of the body. But as the church is

subject to Christ, so also the wives ought to be to their husbands in everything. . . . And let the wife see to it that she respect her husband (Ephesians 5:22-24, 33).

As important as it is for the dancers of the *pas de deux* to follow the explicit directions of the choreographer and to work in harmony with each other, it is far more important for marriage partners to submit to God and work together as "one flesh."

As you may have noticed, I skipped the verses directed to men. That is because mostly women will read this book, and the words addressed to the men are for the men, not for women to use to excuse their own lack of submission. How often I have heard men say, "If only my wife would submit, then I could love her." And how often I have heard women say, "If only my husband would...then I would...." Marriage can move toward its proper order if even one partner will do his or her part. I have seen this principle at work in ballet. A male who is an experienced partner will be able to make up for the deficiencies of an inexperienced female dancer. And an experienced ballerina can compensate for an inexperienced partner. If one decides to do what is right in the relationship, there is far greater opportunity for success in the Lord. If the woman decides to live with her husband in the godly meaning of the word submission, or if the husband decides to love his wife, no matter how unlovable she may be at the moment, God will work, because at least one partner is choosing to act according to God's design.

Even if one partner is not a Christian, God's order for marriage can still apply. At least the one who is a

Christian can do his or her part. During the first century there were many who turned to Christ, but there were also many who were not interested. There were, no doubt, many early Christians who were married to unbelievers, just as there are today. Using the example of Jesus, the apostle Peter spoke to this point.

> While being reviled, He [Jesus] did not revile in return; while suffering, He uttered no threats, but kept entrusting Himself to Him who judges righteously; and He Himself bore our sins in His body on the cross, that we might die to sin and live to righteousness; for by His wounds you were healed (1 Peter 2:23, 24).

> In the same way, you wives, be submissive to your own husbands so that even if any of them are disobedient to the word, they may be won without a word by the behavior of their wives, as they observe your chaste and respectful behavior.

> And let not your adornment be merely external— braiding the hair, and wearing gold jewelry, or putting on dresses; but let it be the hidden person of the heart, with the imperishable quality of a gentle and quiet spirit, which is precious in the sight of God.

> For in this way in former times the holy women also, who hoped in God, used to adorn themselves, being submissive to their own husbands. Thus Sarah obeyed Abraham, calling him lord, and you have become her children if you do what

is right without being frightened by any fear (1 Peter 3:1-6).

Again, Jesus is the example. The words, in the same way as at the beginning of First Peter 3:1, point us back to Jesus. The woman is to behave in the same way that Jesus behaved. This section of Scripture speaks to the woman who has not been treated kindly, because it refers to the passage about how Jesus responded to unjust treatment. The woman is not asked to wait until her husband changes. Rather, she is given examples, instruction, and the ability to obey God.

A woman's submission to her husband is not to depend upon how well he is doing his part in loving her. Rather, her submission is based upon her relationship to the Lord and her obedience to His order for marriage. True submission does not come from a position of weakness. No woman who is weak is submissive. She may be under subjection or oppression, but she is not in submission. Submission is powerful, just like meekness, which has been described as "strength under control." Submission comes from a position of dignity and voluntary choice.

The words *chaste* and *respectful* also describe the godly woman. She is pure in her behavior and in her motives. In other words, she is not using submission as a means to manipulate her husband. Nor has she decided to be submissive for a certain period of time to see if he'll "shape up." Her submission speaks respect loud and clear, and thus her actions will be respectful to her husband.

Respectful behavior not only includes that which is directed toward the husband; it also includes what is said about him in his absence. Blessed is the man who finds a woman like the one in Proverbs 31.

> An excellent wife who can find? For her worth is far above jewels. The heart of her husband trusts in her, and he will have no lack of gain. She does him good and not evil all the days of her life (Proverbs 31:10-12).

Submission, chaste and respectful behavior, and doing good to a husband—in other words, being the partner God has called a woman to be—cannot be performed simply by gritting the teeth. All of these qualities and actions come from an inner heart attitude toward the Lord. This is the "hidden person of the heart, with the imperishable quality of a gentle and quiet spirit, which is precious in the sight of the Lord."

Where might a woman find a gentle and quiet spirit? She cannot find it in her circumstances. Nor can she find it within her own humanity. Such a "hidden person of the heart, with the imperishable quality of a gentle and quiet spirit" can be found only in relationship to Jesus. It is born out of that relationship and is nourished by believing and receiving His love and by spending time in His presence. The "gentle and quiet spirit" comes from being yoked with Him, just as Jesus said:

> Take My yoke upon you, and learn from Me, for I am gentle and humble in heart; and you shall find rest for your souls (Matthew 11:29).

The "gentle and quiet spirit, which is precious in the sight of the Lord" is a reflection of Jesus. This is a quality of "Christ in you, the hope of glory" (Colossians 1:27). A "gentle and quiet spirit" is not striving or contentious. A "gentle and quiet spirit" is a position of strength in the Lord. There is a trust that overturns fear and a peace that stills the storm. It cannot be developed apart from Jesus, for it is found only in Him.

Within the sequence of dances in the *pas de deux* the partners dance together and also separately. The male dancer performs many powerful leaps and stunning turns or jumps. Whereas he is tender and attentive to the woman while partnering her, he displays his power and his own astonishing abilities during his solo. Likewise the woman executes a variety of graceful and difficult steps throughout her solo. Nevertheless, while each dances separately they are still joined in spirit and in intent. The woman waits for the man and he waits for her. They both respect the abilities of the other and appreciate the brief rest while the other performs. When both have completed their solos, they join together again. It is as though they have never left each other. Their unity has not crumbled while they have performed separately. Their relationship is still there in the background to sustain them. I believe that this is the picture of what a marriage should be like, with both partners performing at highest capacity under the leadership of the Lord and in a unity that continues even when they are apart. Neither is submerged; neither is ignored. There is no competition between the two.

Proverbs 31 presents a picture of the truly "liberated woman" in each sequence of the *pas de deux*. First there is a picture of the husband and wife "dancing together" in verses 10 through 12. Then we have the "solos" from verses 13 through 22 and 24 through 27. The brilliance of the woman's performance depends upon her relationship to her husband as well as upon her own talents and diligence. What a picture! Her creativity and ingenuity are not squelched. Neither do they detract her from meeting the physical and emotional needs of her family:

> Her children rise up and bless her; Her husband also, and he praises her, saying: "Many daughters have done nobly, But you excel them all." Charm is deceitful and beauty is vain, but the woman who fears the Lord, she shall be praised. Give her the product of her hands, and let her works praise her in the gates (Proverbs 31:28-31).

The quality of the woman's life comes from her relationship with the Lord.

Communication must also flow forth from our relationship with God. Dancers may easily be injured in the *pas de deux* if they are not completely coordinated in their movements. The communication must be going on at all times, both during rehearsal and on stage. Sometimes during rehearsal the dancers do not include all of the lifts and catches, but just walk through them. This way they learn the sequence and the timing without having to expend all of the energy required in lifts and catches. One afternoon Martin and I were rehearsing together. Somehow I thought we were doing the dance "full out" and he thought we were just walking through it. Consequently I landed on the floor. Martin was totally unprepared to catch me and bear my weight. The look on his face was complete horror. No one was to blame; we simply misunderstood each other. How often this happens in marriage! With no intent of malice or harm there has been some misunderstanding in the miscommunication and someone gets hurt.

When there is miscommunication or misunderstanding in marriage, blame and self-defense lead only to more miscommunication, misunderstanding, and hurt. Therefore, every couple desiring to live by God's design must choose to follow Paul's admonition to all Christians:

> I, therefore, the prisoner of the Lord, entreat you to walk in a manner worthy of the calling with which you have been called, with all humility and gentleness, with patience, showing forbearance to one another in love, being diligent to preserve the unity of the Spirit in the bond of peace. . . . And be kind to one another, tenderhearted, forgiving each other, just as God in Christ also has forgiven you (Ephesians 4:1-3, 32).

Love is costly. Love cost Christ the extreme agony of bearing all the sins of humanity on the cross. Love costs us something of ourselves. Marriage partners need to be prepared and willing to give more than they may receive in the marriage relationship. We have the example of Jesus, who gladly and willingly offered Himself as a sacrifice because of love.

> Therefore be imitators of God, as beloved children; and walk in love, just as Christ also loved you, and gave Himself up for us, an offering and a sacrifice to God as a fragrant aroma (Ephesians 5:1,2).

Love in a marriage relationship is more than romantic feelings. It is more than personal expression and personal satisfaction. Love in marriage is a picture of the relationship of commitment between Christ and His church. The *Grand Pas de Deux* of the universe is the Dance of Love and commitment between Christ and His bride. Every other Christian *pas de deux* is to reflect the majesty, dignity, beauty, and devotion of the *Grand Pas de Deux*.

> Wives, be subject to your own husbands, as to the Lord. For the husband is the head of the wife, as Christ also is the head of the church, He Himself being the Savior of the body But as the church is subject to Christ, so also the wives ought to be to their husbands in everything.

> Husbands, love your wives, just as Christ also loved the church and gave Himself up for her; that He might sanctify her, having cleansed her by the washing of water with the word, that He might present to Himself the church in all her glory, having no spot or wrinkle or any such thing; but that she should be holy and blameless.

> So husbands ought also to love their own wives as their own bodies. He who loves his own wife loves himself; for no one ever hated his own flesh, but nourishes and cherishes it, just as Christ also does the church, because we are members of His body.

> For this cause a man shall leave his father and mother, and shall cleave to his wife; and the two shall become one flesh. This mystery is great; but I am speaking with reference to Christ and the church. Nevertheless let each individual among you also love his own wife even as himself; and let the wife see to it that she respect her husband (Ephesians 5:22-33).

Marriage is an honorable state. It is no place for petty quarrels, selfishness, or unreasonable demands. God designed the *pas de deux* to reflect His love in relationship. He created the marriage bonds for the fruit of the Spirit as well as for bearing children. May we devote ourselves to doing our part in reflecting the Lord with every step we take in whatever dance He casts us, in the *pas de deux*, in the solo, or in the *corps de ballet.*

Devotional Exercise

1. Read Ephesians 5:22-33; 1 Peter 2:23, 24; and 1 Peter 3:1-6. Describe the kind of submission that a loving Father has designed for a godly wife. What are some of the misunderstandings about submission that foster rebellion?

2. Read Proverbs 31:10-31. What details about this description demonstrate the woman's submissive attitude?

3. Read Titus 2:3-5 and 1 Corinthians 13:4-8. How might you express love to your husband?

14

The Performance: Serving God and Bearing Fruit

What intricacies of movement,
what nuances of grace,
has my Choreographer designed
for a soaring spirit suspended in an aging body?

My *pirouettes* are not as sure,
nor high the *grand jeté*.
Yet some fluidity of life
penetrates my *port de bras*,
and a subdued arabesque reminisces
yesterday's brilliant extension.
No more frolic of *Coppelia*
nor spell of *Swan Lake*.
Bluebird wings from *Sleeping Beauty*
gather dust in the closet.
Satin shoes pressed against booties
recall the former dances—

romantic interlude,
the dance of motherhood, fatherhood,
new variations of *pas de deux,*
intricate interweavings into *pas de trois*
the dance ever expanding.

Children dance into maturity,
another pas de deux.

Familiar patterns, familiar steps,
echo dances of former days—
changement, bourrée, relevé,
balancé, glissade,
kaleidoscopic designs;
no repeat performances,
for the dance is never the same.

I hear the overture:
A New Dance has begun.

The anticipation of performance is felt in every sinew as the dancers stand waiting in the wings. The orchestra in the pit is playing the overture. Dancers test their shoes and move a bit to relax. With acute physical and mental alertness they wait, ready to perform the dance. Besides the years of preparation, they have spent numerous rehearsal hours practicing each sequence of steps. They have reviewed the dance in their minds before going to sleep at night, and they have practiced over and over again. Now is the time to present their gift of creativity Every time a ballet is performed the final touches of creativity come forth. The same is true for any performing artist. The final point of creativity is in the performing, whether it be music, drama, or ballet.

Ballet is not simply a process without a goal. Every class is geared to performance—every correction, every accomplishment. Although we are in process as we grow in our Christian walk, we also desire to bear fruit. We too have goals of service for the Lord. Christianity is more than self-improvement; it is not just to make us feel better. No, we have been called to serve. Christianity is the performance of Christ s will to bear eternal fruit. Our performance is not for personal gain; it is to fulfill God's plans for building His kingdom. Again, Jesus is our example. He came not to be served, but to serve.

After a couple of years of college, a young friend of ours attended a Bible school in New Zealand. The time was rich in both learning and ministry. At the end of the year of Bible school, he returned to the United States to complete college. He got a part-time job in a Christian bookstore and hoped to have opportunities to continue serving the Lord. About a month after he was home, we asked him if he had experienced any "culture shock" when he went abroad. He looked at us for a moment and confessed that he was having a difficult time adjusting to the self- centered atmosphere in the United States. He said that in New Zealand the young people yearned to serve God. Their burning question was, "How can I serve God more?" Here, he lamented, the pervading question seems to be: "What else is God going to do for me?"

The high call into service with Christ has far greater implications and far greater results than any ballet performance will ever hope to achieve. Yet, I see dancers who have given themselves to ballet far more than many Christians have given themselves to serving God. Perhaps part of the reason is that we limit the idea of service to some particular form of professionalism: of being a pastor of a church, a teacher in a seminary or Bible college, or a missionary on foreign soil. Opportunities to serve God are avail- able and waiting just where we might be. We do not need a stage set or ballet or an orchestra in the pit. Our stage is the place where God puts us, and we move by the sound of His voice to our innermost being.

For many women service begins in the home and extends abroad. Furthermore, God calls us to different forms of service in the various seasons of our lives. Fruit bearing is to begin at new birth and to continue until we meet our Lord face-to-face at the end of the life we now know here. Fruit bearing may occur in the family, the neighborhood, the church, and the world. God assigns the roles and He creates the dances.

Even if a dancer performs a solo dance, she is part of an entire whole during performance. She is part of a company under the leadership of an artistic director. The artistic director also follows the directions of the choreographer, the one who has created the dances. The ballet company operates much like a single unit, a body.

God formed the body of believers to function as a single unit, with each person fulfilling an essential part.

> There are varieties of gifts, but the same Spirit. And there are varieties of ministries, and the same Lord. And there are varieties of effects, but the same God who works all things in all persons. But to each one is given the manifestation of

the Spirit for the common good (1 Corinthians 12:4-7).

Ministries are given for the sake of the body rather than for the enhancement of the individual. One ministry, however important as it may seem, does not diminish the importance of any other ministry.

> One and the same Spirit works all these things, distributing to each one individually just as He wills. For even as the body is one and yet has many members, and all the members of the body, though they are many, are one body, so also is Christ. For by one Spirit we were all baptized into one body, whether Jews or Greeks, whether slaves or free, and we were all made to drink of one Spirit.
>
> For the body is not one member, but many. If the foot should say, "Because I am not a hand, I am not a part of the body," it is not for this reason any the less a part of the body
>
> And if the ear should say, "Because I am not an eye, I am not a part of the body," it is not for this reason any the less a part of the body. If the whole body were an eye, where would the hearing be? If the whole were hearing, where would the sense of smell be? But now God has placed the members, each one of them, in the body, just as He desired (1 Corinthians 12:11-18).

Some ministries are seen by crowds. Others are hidden away in prayer and quiet service.

For every stunning performance before large crowds at the ballet, there are also many hidden persons who contribute their own expertise and skill for the performance: company teachers, rehearsal directors, musicians, financial backers, technical directors and designers, costumers, makeup artists, stage crews, technicians, and promotional and publicity personnel. The same is true in Christian service. Not all areas of service are as visible as others. Some may not look as important, but they are all absolutely vital to the work of the body.

Every member of the body of Christ has an essential function in the building up of the body:

> ...until we all attain to the unity of the faith, and of the knowledge of the Son of God, to a mature man, to the measure of the stature which belongs to the fulness of Christ...from whom the whole body, being fitted and held together by that which every joint supplies, according to the proper working of each individual part, causes the growth of the body for the building up of itself in love (Ephesians 4:13,16).

Yet, there is a tendency to look at the dances of others and wish we could dance those dances instead of our own. Jealous looks and envious yearnings fill the breasts of many dancers who stand among the *corps de ballet* in the wings as they watch the soloists perform. How easy it is to look at how God is using other Christians and wish we had that talent, training, and call upon our lives! But God has warned against this:

> We are not bold to class or compare ourselves
> with some of those who commend themselves;
> but when they measure themselves by themselves,
> and compare themselves with themselves, they
> are without understanding (2 Corinthians 10:12).

Disobedience to this verse also prevents some people from serving because they compare themselves with others who are successful. They say, "I can't," to God and fall into the trap of the servant who was given one talent instead of two or ten. Instead of serving God with the one talent, he hid it away for fear of losing the little he had.

There is not a single Christian who is not called, gifted, and equipped to serve. Peter admonished:

> As each one has received a special gift, employ
> it in serving one another, as good stewards of the
> manifold grace of God. Whoever speaks, let him
> speak, as it were, the utterances of God; whoever
> serves, let him do so as by the strength which
> God supplies; so that in all things God may be
> glorified through Jesus Christ, to whom belongs
> the glory and dominion forever and ever. Amen
> (1 Peter 4:10,11).

Every Christian is called to glorify God in service. Every Christian is a member of the "company." All have appointed roles and duties for service. Paul considered ministry to be a gift of God's grace rather than merely a duty to be done. That is why he called ministries gifts. They are indeed gifts, because it is a special privilege to be allowed to participate in what God is doing.

Performance of good works must also be kept in proper perspective. Service is not the way into salvation, but the response.

> We are His workmanship, created in Christ Jesus for good works, which God prepared beforehand, that we should walk in them (Ephesians 2:10).

Paul listed some of these works of service in Romans 12 right after he urged believers to present themselves to God for service in the spirit of humility.

> Since we have gifts that differ according to the grace given to us, let each exercise them accordingly; if prophecy, according to the proportion of his faith; if service, in his serving; or he who teaches, in his teaching; or he who exhorts, in his exhortation; he who gives, with liberality; he who leads, with diligence; he who shows mercy, with cheerfulness (Romans 12:6-8).

The Lord showed me such a gracious picture of my own ministry. I had given a little broom to our daughter when she was three years old. With great seriousness she helped me sweep the kitchen. She wanted to do what I did and she wanted to help me. She was a joy to my heart even though she missed the crumbs and the dust. Likewise the Lord allows me to do what I see Him do, and He allows me to participate in His actions. He rejoices at my participation in spite of my human failings. He looks beyond the "crumbs and dust" and brings forth His fruit. True Christian service comes from relationship with the Father and moves toward His perfect will being accomplished through imperfect vessels.

Service does not truly reflect the Father if there is any pride. Although serving God is a high calling, it can only be accomplished through humility.

> Consider your calling, brethren, that there were not many wise according to the flesh, not many mighty, not many noble; but God has chosen the foolish things of the world to shame the wise, and God has chosen the weak things of the world to shame the things which are strong, and the base things of the world and the despised, God has chosen, the things that are not, that He might nullify the things that are, that no man should boast before God.

> But by His doing you are in Christ Jesus, who became to us wisdom from God, and righteousness and sanctification, and redemption, that, just as it is written, "Let him who boasts, boast in the Lord" (1 Corinthians 1:26-31).

Pride can destroy a ministry because it does not fit well with love or with the work of the Holy Spirit. Peter calls believers to—

> …clothe yourselves with humility toward one another, for God is opposed to the proud, but gives grace to the humble. Humble yourselves, therefore, under the mighty hand of God, that He may exalt you at the proper time, casting all your anxiety upon Him, because He cares for you (1 Peter 5:5-7).

Humility does not look at the self and say, "I can do this," or, "I can't do that." Humility looks at God and says, "I can do all things through Him who strengthens me" (Philippians 4:13). "Faithful is He who calls you, and He also will bring it to pass" (1 Thessalonians 5:24). Blaise Pascal advised:

> Do little things as if they were great, because of the majesty of the Lord Jesus Christ who dwells in thee; and do great things as if they were little and easy, because of His omnipotence.

Along with humility Paul lists other attitudes which are evident in godly service:

> Be devoted to one another in brotherly love; give preference to one another in honor; not lagging behind in diligence, fervent in spirit, serving the Lord; rejoicing in hope, persevering in tribulation, devoted to prayer, contributing to the needs of the saints, practicing hospitality (Romans 12:10-13).

Love is the hallmark of Christian service.

Each of us will find a place of service, but again we have to be careful not to think that God will call us to do exactly what the next person is doing. The variety of ways to serve matches perfectly the variety of God's children. I had a friend who was very gifted by the Lord, but who was quite different from other women who eagerly served the Lord. One day I wrote a little parable for her. It went this way.

Once upon a time there was a prince who had a lovely strawberry patch next to a wooded glade. A solitary violet grew nearby. Every day the prince came to visit the patch to eat strawberries and to gaze upon the graceful beauty of the violet. The strawberries busily produced fruit and often chided the violet because she was different and because she did not bear any food for the fine young prince. For a while the violet tried desperately to look like the strawberries. She tried to act like them, too, and twisted a leaf and nearly choked a petal. Finally she began to droop. She wished she could just disappear into the ground.

The prince noticed that the violet's countenance had changed. He asked if she were ill, but she just inwardly wept. She so desired to give a worthy gift to the prince. The prince knelt down close to the violet and she felt a warm drop of water splash upon her leaf. As she looked up at the prince, he said, "Every day I look forward to coming here and feasting my eyes upon you. The intricacy of your design, the delicacy of your color, the rhythm of your response to a breeze, and your quiet beauty bring peace to my soul and joy to my heart."

"But I'm not like the strawberries. I have no food to give you, sweet prince," replied the violet.

"Of course you're not like the strawberries. You were not made to feed my flesh, but my spirit," he answered.

That night the violet dreamed she was in a field of violets and that there was one lone strawberry plant. She knew the prince loved strawberries and would cherish this one's rare fruit. When she awoke, she stretched up toward the sun and waited for her prince with hope and expectancy. At last she knew that she too had something to give to the prince.

I remember another story told by a radio preacher. When some Christians were pressuring a mother of three young children to become active in an organized form of Christian service, she responded by saying, "Someday in heaven there will be three pairs of eyes looking at me." She knew the work that God had given her for that period of her life. Christian service in the home is not a lowly calling. Here are the lives we can most influence for Christ. Here are the charges He has given us to nurture, to teach, and to discipline. Even older women are to instruct and encourage younger women in their service to the Lord in the home.

> Older women likewise are to be reverent in their behavior, not malicious gossips, nor enslaved to much wine, teaching what is good, that they may encourage the young women to love their husbands, to love their children, to be sensible, pure, workers at home, kind, being subject to their own husbands, that the word of God may not be dishonored (Titus 2:3-5).

"Workers at home" does not limit the scope of ministry, but it does indicate that housework and rearing children are all part of ministry to the Lord. Some have mistaken this verse to mean that women must be only in the home and not at all in the workplace, but Proverbs 31 lists all kinds of service both inside and outside the home.

One of the most famous sayings in theatre arts is: "There are no small parts, only small actors." As much as actors may balk at this, they discover that it's true. A person who regards a role to be too small for him is truly a small actor. On the other hand, it's a joy to see excellent actors and actresses make even small parts come alive. I often watch those with small parts to see if they are staying "in character" while simply standing on stage.

In God's service there are no small parts, only small actors. Every aspect of service for His kingdom is worthy of our very best. Just as play directors watch what young actors and actresses do with small parts, the Lord watches what we do with small bits of service. After He has given us something to do, no matter how small or large, we want Him to say:

> Well done, good and faithful slave; you were faithful with a few things, I will put you in charge of many things; enter into the joy of your master (Matthew 25:21).

The more we choose to serve Him instead of ourselves, the more He works in us to accomplish His will. This is not for our own sense of significance, but rather for fulfilling His plan to perform His will on earth through His body, which is made up of every true disciple of Christ.

> To everyone who has shall more be given, and he shall have an abundance; but from the one who does not have, even what he does have shall be taken away (Matthew 25:29).

Not only is more given in terms of opportunities and in terms of His abundant supply, but more dedication and faithfulness in service are required by the Master. However, He expects no more from us than what He Himself has already supplied.

> From everyone who has been given much shall much be required; and to whom they entrusted much, of him they will ask all the more (Luke 12:48).

Service to God does not originate from within our own limited human selves. Although God may use the natural talents He has already given us, fruitfulness in service comes from His life within the believer and from His anointing for service. His anointing is His appointment or assignment to a particular task. His anointing is also the Holy Spirit within us to enable us to serve Him.

> God, who said, "Light shall shine out of darkness," is the One who has shone in our hearts to give the light of the knowledge of the glory of God in the face of Christ. But we have this treasure in earthen vessels, that the surpassing greatness of the power may be of God and not from ourselves (2 Corinthians 4:6, 7).

We are simply vessels for service, but we desire to be the kind of vessels He can use.

> In a large house there are not only gold and silver vessels, but also vessels of wood and of earthenware, and some to honor and some to dishonor. Therefore, if a man cleanses himself from these things, he will be a vessel for honor, sanctified, useful to the Master, prepared for every good work (2 Timothy 2:20, 21).

The spiritual condition of the vessel is important. God evaluates service on the basis of our faithfulness to do His will rather than on results seen by the human eye.

Therefore, even in the midst of conflict and persecution, and even when many opposed his preaching, Paul could thank God that He was leading him in triumph.

Fruitfulness and apparent success are not always synonymous. A young couple served as Wycliffe missionaries in Nepal for five years. During that time they learned a tribal language, put it into a written language, and translated the Gospel of Mark and part of Genesis. They had only two converts before Wycliffe was required to leave the country. One convert remained faithful; the other went back to the religion of his tribe. The one who remained faithful has suffered great persecution among his people. From worldly measurements we might think that the five years ended in failure. But from God's standpoint, His work does not fail. His people were faithful to do what He had called them to do. Therefore they could also say with Paul:

> Thanks be to God, who always leads us in His triumph in Christ, and manifests through us the sweet aroma of the knowledge of Him in every place. For we are a fragrance of Christ to God among those who are being saved and among those who are perishing; to the one an aroma from death to death, to the other an aroma from life to life. And who is adequate for these things? For we are not like many, peddling the word of God, but as from sincerity but as from God, we speak in Christ in the sight of God (2 Corinthians 2:14-17).

We do triumph when we serve Him in His way for He is faithful.

Mary Lewer, our missionary friend who rode to church with us for a number of years, continued bearing fruit in old age. Although she was not able to serve in the same way as she had in China, she devoted her time to prayer and to making little stuffed toys for children. She took great delight in these simple tasks. However, it was her manner of living and her conversation that was most fruitful in the lives of those around her. She stimulated faith. She patiently endured without complaint. She planted seeds in the lives of our children. She lived until she was 93, and she was never too old to serve Jesus. She was an example to me, so that when I reached the ominous age of 50, I considered the two ways a woman could possibly go, and then wrote this poem.

Two Women at Fifty

Empty,
she wonders
what is left
from all the giving,
comes up short
without supply,
searches for water
in clouds of dust.

Her power
to nurture and sustain
fades
in the bleach of many suns,
and

she is left
hanging on the line
dry.

Filled,
she wonders
at His depth of supply,
filling the giving,
never running dry,
with arms outstretched
in latter rain
of latter years

Her power
to nurture and sustain
surges
from the light of one Son,
and
she lives
to be poured out
for Him.

Paul never planned to retire from serving the Lord. He continued to press forward. Even under great adversity he rejoiced in the privilege of bearing fruit.

> Therefore we do not lose heart, but though our outer man is decaying, yet our inner man is being renewed day by day. For momentary, light affliction is producing for us an eternal weight of glory far beyond all comparison, while we look

not at the things which are seen, but at the things which are not seen; for the things which are seen are temporal, but the things which are not seen are eternal (2 Corinthians 4:16-18).

Ballet dancers have been known to break bones during performance and to continue anyway. They are sometimes in pain with pulled muscles or bleeding toes, or with some kind of illness that will just have to wait. They do all of this with no eternal glory waiting for them at the end of the dance—only the applause of a crowd that may soon forget them. Yet their devotion and faithfulness to ballet stand as examples to us who have a far greater reason for devotion and faithfulness.

Furthermore, dancers cannot continue indefinitely. Their days of performance are numbered. They give it all they can as long as they can. On the other hand, followers of Christ will continue on eternally. Although the days of service here on earth in our mortal bodies are numbered, we have the promise of eternity with immortal bodies and with uninterrupted relationship with our Lord. Perhaps what we do here is merely a training ground for an eternity of serving God. We have a greater Choreographer and a greater Dance which will continue forever.

As the ballet reaches the *grand finale*, the dancers enter for their last dance. The performance ends with great flourish and excitement, and the curtain drops. As applause drowns out the final strains of music, the curtain opens again. The dancers return for curtain calls, elegant curtsies, and deep bows. Shouts of "Bravo!" pierce the air and flowers flood the stage. The glorious sense of accomplishment and goodwill warms hearts with the recognition of "Well done!"

As our dance with the Lord nears the Grand Finale, we have an audience and a destiny.

> Therefore, since we have so great a cloud of witnesses surrounding us, let us also lay aside every encumbrance, and the sin which so easily entangles us, and let us run with endurance the race that is set before us, fixing our eyes on Jesus, the author and perfecter of faith, who for the joy set before Him endured the cross, despising the shame, and has sat down at the right hand of the throne of God (Hebrews 12:1, 2).

The finale into eternity will begin as Jesus receives us to Himself. Instead of "Bravo," He will say, "Well done, my daughter." Instead of flowers He will crown us with the crown of righteousness and the incorruptible crown of life. Then we will humbly bow before Him, cast our crowns at His feet, and sing:

> Worthy art Thou, our Lord and our God, to receive glory and honor and power; for Thou didst create all things, and because of Thy will they existed, and were created (Revelation 4:11).

> Worthy is the Lamb that was slain to receive power and riches and wisdom and might and honor and glory and blessing (Revelation 5:12).

Ballet Magnificat!
"America's Premier Christian Ballet Company"

Throughout this book I have used ballet as an extended analogy of the Christian walk. *Ballet Magnificat!* ballet company members beautifully combine the two as they use their God-given talents to share the Gospel around the world. They are dancers who are also walking with Christ, or perhaps I should say: Dancing with Christ, just as David danced before the Ark! They are Christians who take their Christianity seriously and who share their faith openly as they present the Gospel message and give personal testimonies.

Ballet Magnificat! was formed in 1986, one year before the first publishing of this book under the title *Lord of the Dance: The Beauty of the Disciplined Life.* Prior to that, Kathy Thibodeaux, the Artistic Director, had danced with Ballet Mississippi and won a silver medal at the II USA International Ballet Competition in 1982. She and her husband, Keith, and their very able staff have worked assiduously in developing their dancers physically, artistically, and spiritually through these past thirty-one years. Kathy continues to dance, choreograph, and inspire both students and company members.

233

You will be delighted with their stunning performances on their website, which also details their Mission, Statement of Faith, travel, and work. As I viewed their video clips I was drawn back to the joy and beauty of ballet and further encouraged in my own walk with the Lord. Please visit them at http://www.balletmagnificat. com.

May God bless you as you seek to walk/dance by grace through faith and serve Him wherever He has placed you.

Deidre Bobgan

November, 2017

Made in the USA
Monee, IL
04 March 2023

29088078R10134